EASY GUITAR WITH NOTES & TAB

The Best of Jim Croce

T0034086

Cover photo by Paul Wilson

ISBN-13: 978-0-634-01384-3

HAL•LEONARD®
CORPORATION
7777 W. BLUEMOUND RD. P.O. BOX 13819 MILWAUKEE, WI 53213

Visit Hal Leonard Online at
www.halleonard.com

STRUM AND PICK PATTERNS

This chart contains the suggested strum and pick patterns that are referred to by number at the beginning of each song in this book. The symbols ⊓ and ∨ in the strum patterns refer to down and up strokes, respectively. The letters in the pick patterns indicate which right-hand fingers plays which strings.

p = thumb
i = index finger
m = middle finger
a = ring finger

For example; Pick Pattern 2
is played: thumb - index - middle - ring

Strum Patterns   Pick Patterns

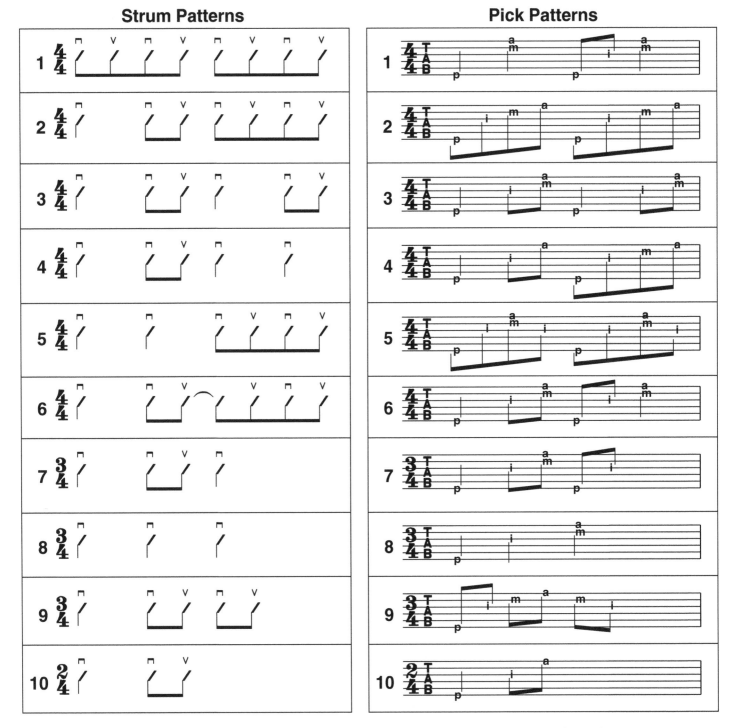

You can use the 3/4 Strum or Pick Patterns in songs written in compound meter (6/8, 9/8, 12/8, etc.).
For example, you can accompany a song in 6/8 by playing the 3/4 pattern twice in each measure.
The 4/4 Strum and Pick Patterns can be used for songs written in cut time (¢) by doubling the note
time values in the patterns. Each pattern would therefore last two measures in cut time.

Age

Words and Music by Jim Croce and Ingrid Croce

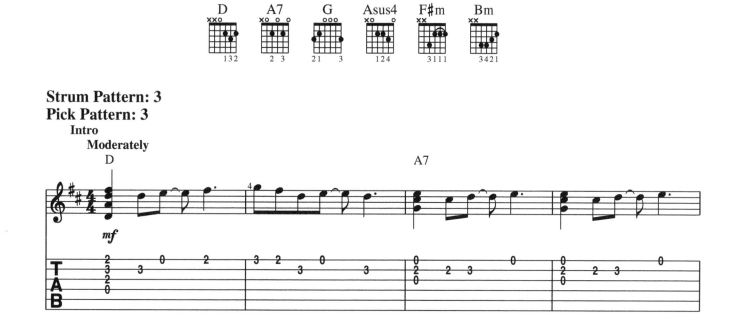

Strum Pattern: 3
Pick Pattern: 3

Intro
Moderately

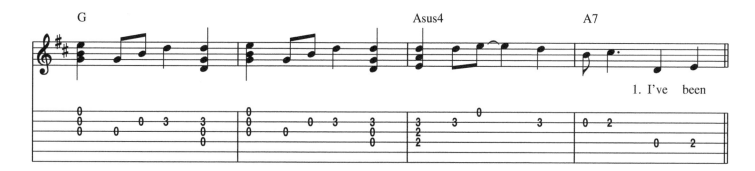

Verse

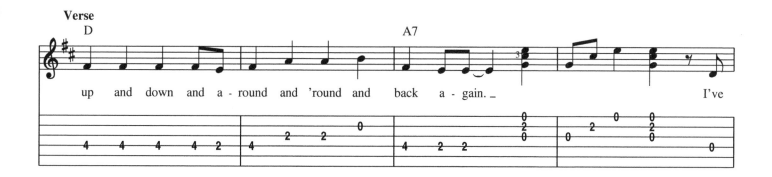

up and down and a-round and 'round and back a-gain. __ I've

been so man-y plac-es I can't re-mem-ber where __ or when. And my on-ly boss was the

clock on the wall and my on - ly friend _____ nev - er real - ly was _

_ a friend _ at all. I've trad - ed love for pen - nies,

%. **Chorus**

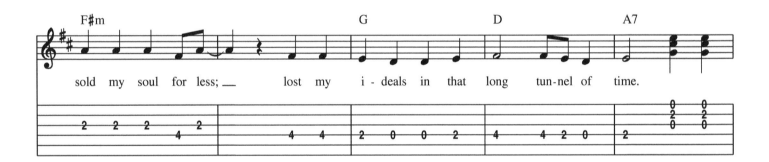

sold my soul for less; _ lost my i - deals in that long tun-nel of time.

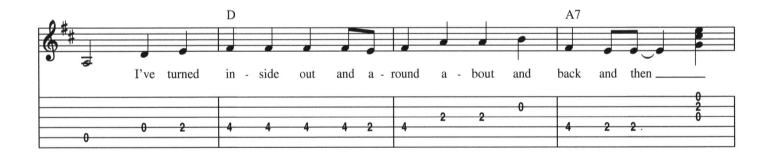

I've turned in - side out and a - round a - bout and back and then _____

To Coda ⊕

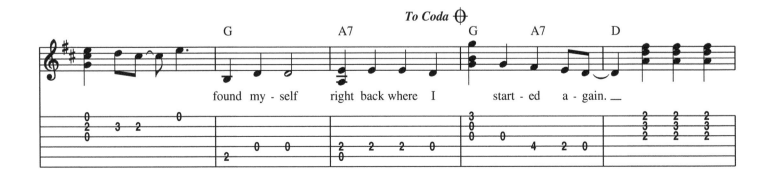

found my - self right back where I start - ed a - gain. _

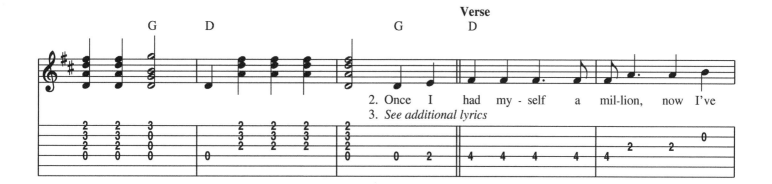

2. Once I had my - self a mil - lion, now I've
3. *See additional lyrics*

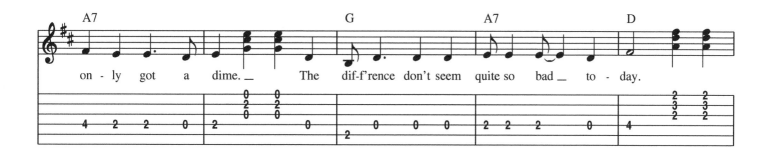

on - ly got a dime. _ The dif - f'rence don't seem quite so bad _ to - day.

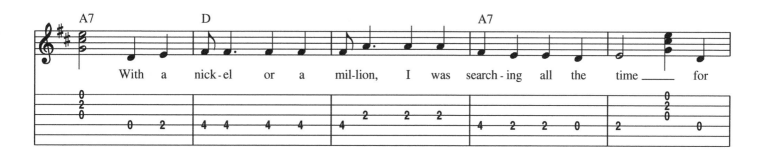

With a nick - el or a mil - lion, I was search - ing all the time _____ for

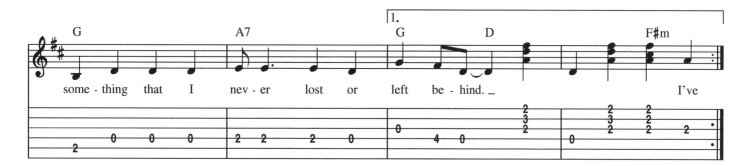

some - thing that I nev - er lost or left be - hind. _ I've

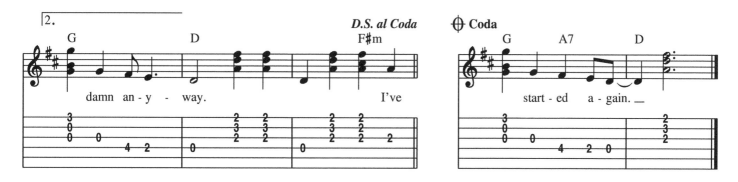

damn an - y - way. I've   start - ed a - gain. _

Additional Lyrics

3. Now I'm in my second circle and I'm headed for the top,
I've learned a lot of things along the way.
I'll be careful when I'm climbin' 'cause it hurts a lot to drop,
And when you're down nobody gives a damn anyway.

Another Day Another Town

Words and Music by Jim Croce

Strum Pattern: 4
Pick Pattern: 1

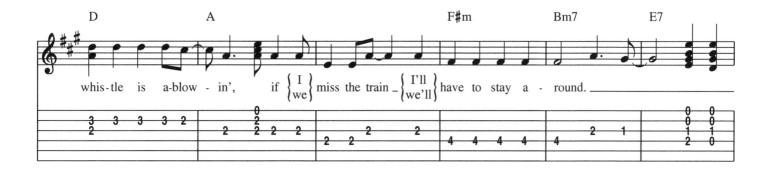

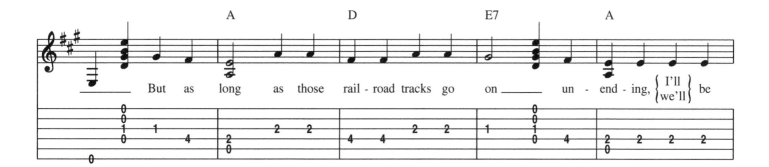

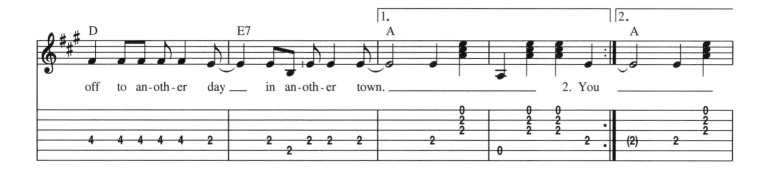

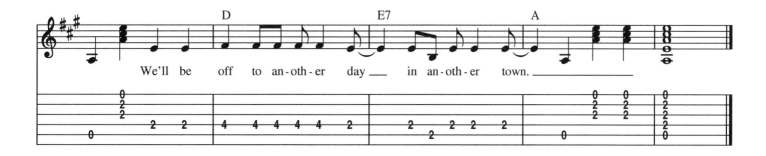

Additional Lyrics

2. You say you'd like to ramble with me,
   This ain't no life for a girl,
   Too many people out to get you
   In a hobo's world.
   And it gets mighty cold when you're on the road,
   'Cause a boxcar never was a home,
   But you could join me if you want,
   I'm gettin' mighty tired of bein' alone.

Bad, Bad Leroy Brown

Words and Music by Jim Croce

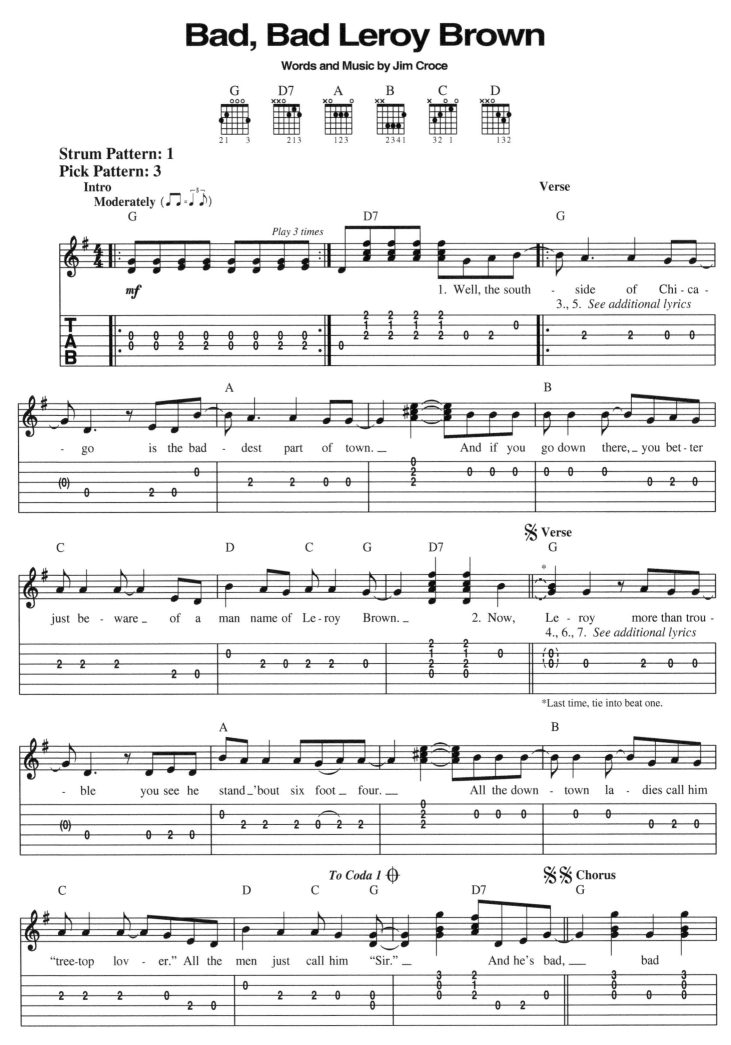

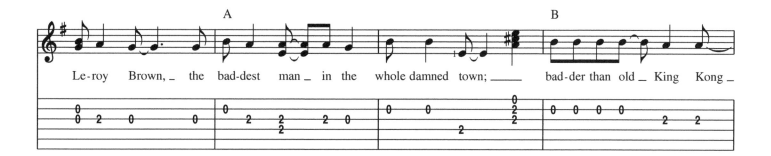

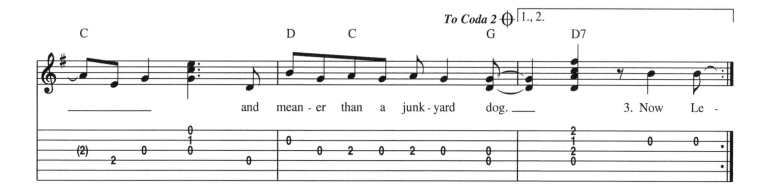

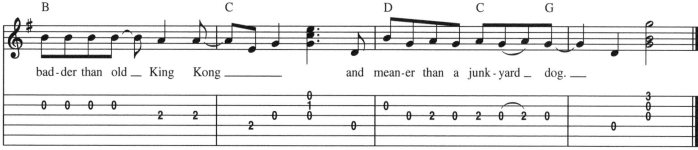

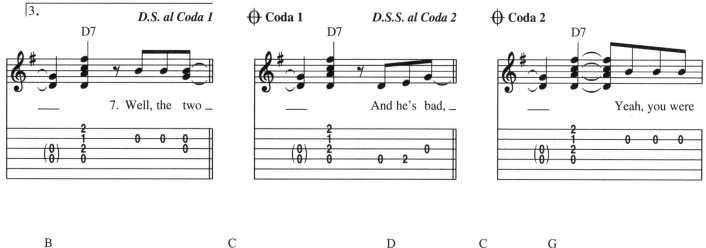

Additional Lyrics

3. Now Leroy, he a gambler
   And he like his fancy clothes
   And he like to wave
   His diamond rings
   In front of ev'rybody's nose.

4. He got a custom Continental,
   He got a Eldorado, too;
   He got a thirty-two gun
   In his pocket for fun,
   He's got a razor in his shoe.

5. Well, Friday 'bout a week ago,
   Leroy shootin' dice,
   And at the edge of the bar
   Sat a girl name of Doris,
   And oh, that girl looked nice.

6. Well, he cast his eyes upon her,
   And the trouble soon began,
   And Leroy Brown,
   He learned a lesson 'bout messin'
   With the wife of a jealous man.

7. Well, the two men took to fightin',
   And when they pulled them from the floor
   Leroy looked
   Like a jigsaw puzzle
   With a couple of pieces gone.

Big Wheel

Words and Music by Jim Croce

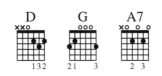

Strum Pattern: 1
Pick Pattern: 2

Intro
Brightly

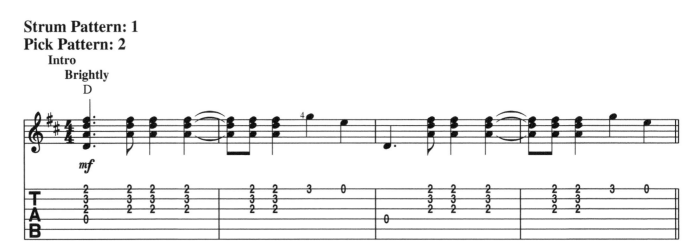

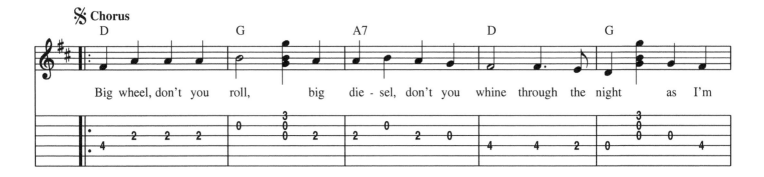

Big wheel, don't you roll, big die - sel, don't you whine through the night as I'm

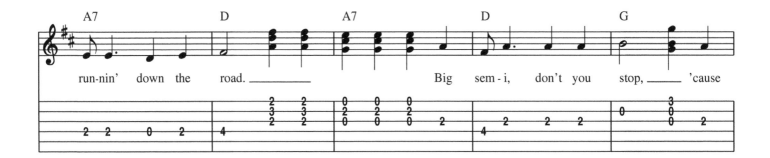

run-nin' down the road. _____ Big sem - i, don't you stop, _____ 'cause

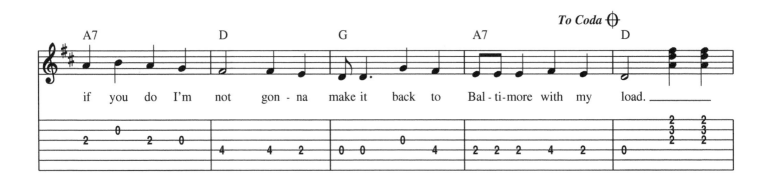

if you do I'm not gon - na make it back to Bal - ti-more with my load. _____

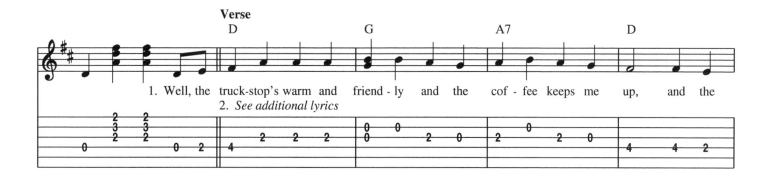

Verse

1. Well, the truck-stop's warm and friend - ly and the cof - fee keeps me up, and the
2. *See additional lyrics*

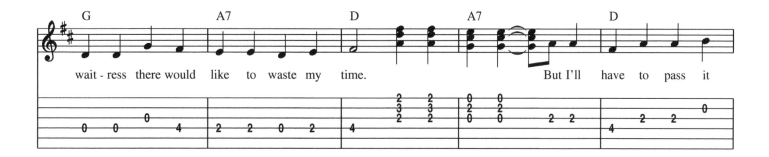

wait - ress there would like to waste my time. But I'll have to pass it

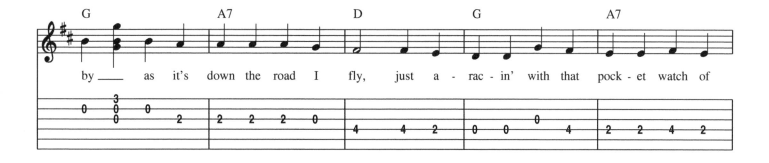

by ___ as it's down the road I fly, just a - rac - in' with that pock - et watch of

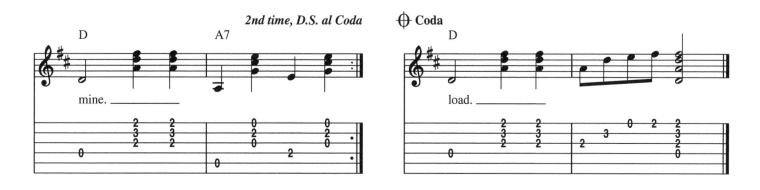

2nd time, D.S. al Coda   Coda

mine. ___   load. ___

Additional Lyrics

2. Smoke a-puffin', tires a hummin',
   Burnin' up the road,
   Countin' road signs and the miles to Baltimore.
   One eye out for weighin' stations,
   One for radar traps,
   They can't stop me, 'cause my plans don't call for that.

Hard Time Losin' Man

Words and Music by Jim Croce

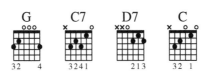

Strum Pattern: 1, 3
Pick Pattern: 2, 4

Intro
Moderately

And you think you've seen

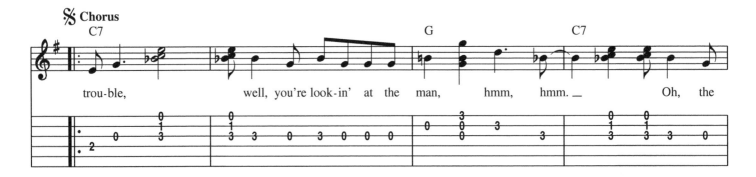

trou-ble, well, you're look-in' at the man, hmm, hmm. ___ Oh, the

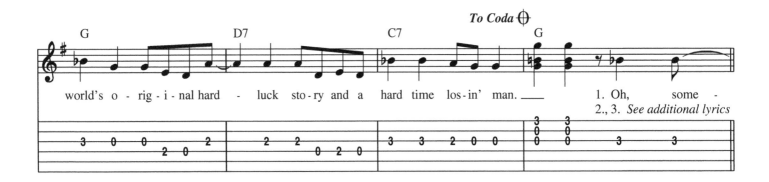

world's o - rig - i - nal hard - luck sto-ry and a hard time los-in' man. ___ 1. Oh, some - 2., 3. *See additional lyrics*

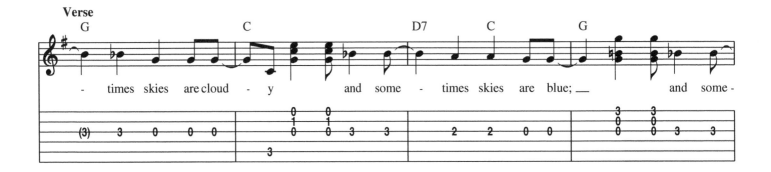

- times skies are cloud - y and some - times skies are blue; ___ and some-

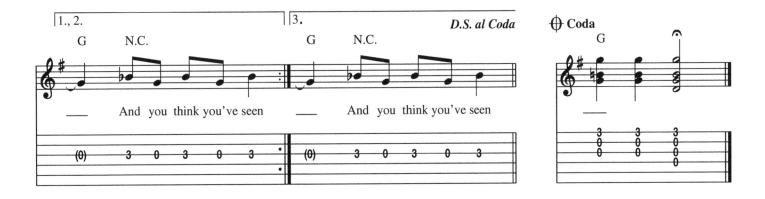

Additional Lyrics

2. Oh, I saved up all my money,
   I gonna buy me a flashy car;
   So I go downtown to see the man,
   And he smokin' on a big cigar.
   Well, he must a' thought I was Rockefeller,
   Or an uptown man of wealth;
   He said, "Boy I got the car that's made for you,
   And it's cleaner than the Board of Health."
   Then I get on the highway, oh, I feelin' fine, I hit a bump
   Then I found I bought a car held together by wire,
   And a couple a' hunks of twine.

3. Oh, Friday night, feelin' right
   I head out on the street;
   Standin' in the doorway
   Was a dealer known as Pete.
   Well, he sold me a dime of some super-fine
   Dynamite from Mexico.
   I spent all that night
   Just tryin' to get right
   On an ounce of oregano.

Hey Tomorrow

Words and Music by Jim Croce

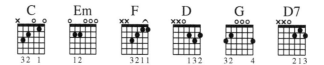

Strum Pattern: 1, 3
Pick Pattern: 2, 4

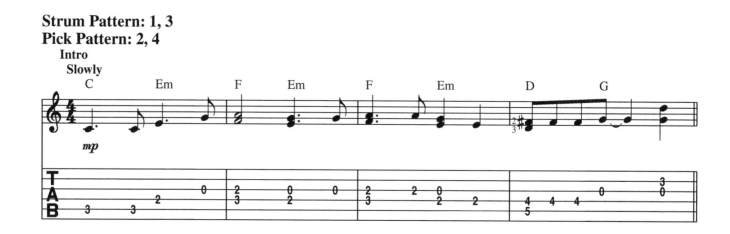

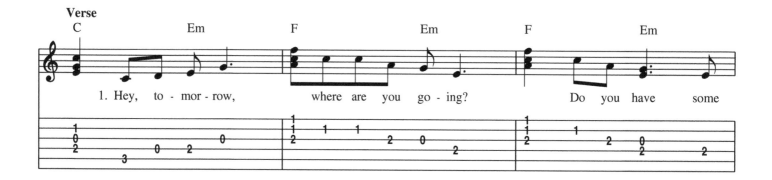

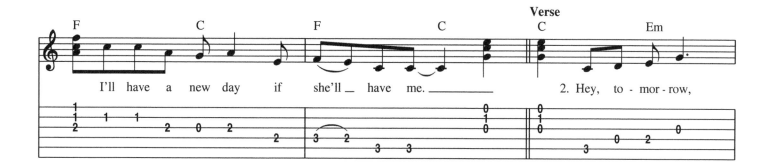

I'll have a new day if she'll __ have me. _____ 2. Hey, to-mor-row,

I can't show you noth-ing. You've seen it all pass by your door. _____

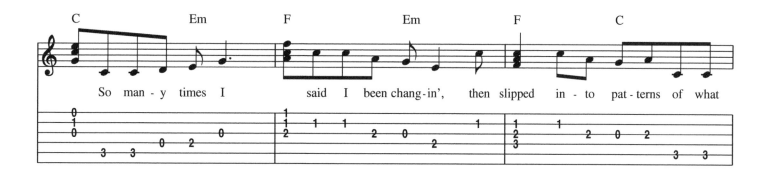

So man-y times I said I been chang-in', then slipped in-to pat-terns of what

Bridge

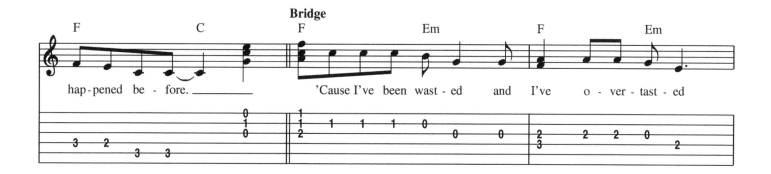

hap-pened be-fore. _____ 'Cause I've been wast-ed and I've o-ver-tast-ed

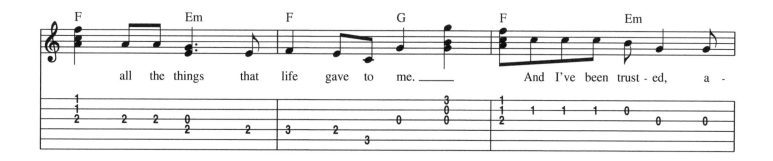

all the things that life gave to me. _____ And I've been trust-ed, a-

bused and bust - ed, and I've been tak - en by those close to

Verse

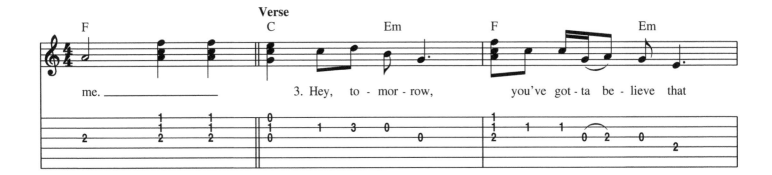

me. _____ 3. Hey, to - mor - row, you've got - ta be - lieve that

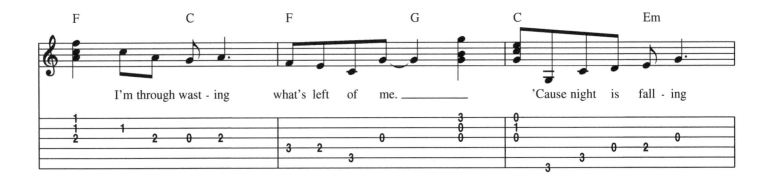

I'm through wast - ing what's left of me. _____ 'Cause night is fall - ing

and the dawn _ is call - ing; I'll have a new day if she'll _ have me. __

I'll Have to Say I Love You in a Song

Words and Music by Jim Croce

Strum Pattern: 4
Pick Pattern: 4

Intro
Moderately

1. Well, I

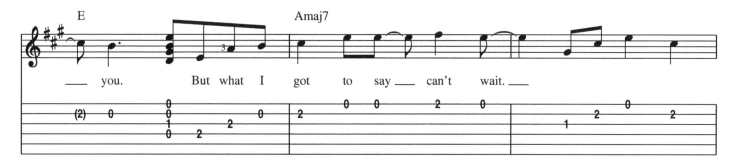

know it's kind of late. ___ I hope I did-n't wake ___

2., 3. *See additional lyrics*

you. But what I got to say ___ can't wait. ___

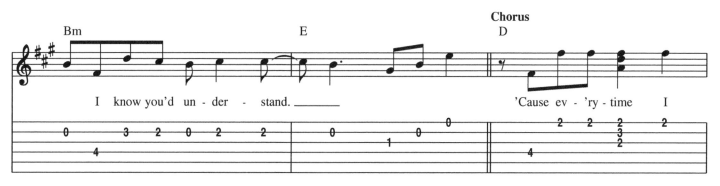

I know you'd un-der-stand. _____ 'Cause ev-'ry-time I

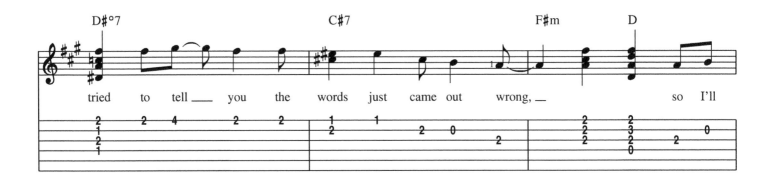

tried to tell ___ you the words just came out wrong, ___ so I'll

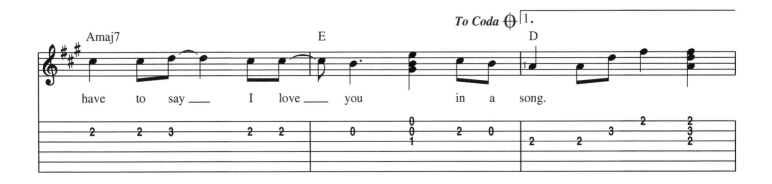

To Coda ⊕ |1.

have to say ___ I love ___ you in a song.

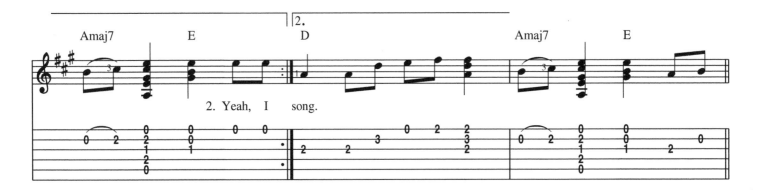

|2.

2. Yeah, I song.

Interlude

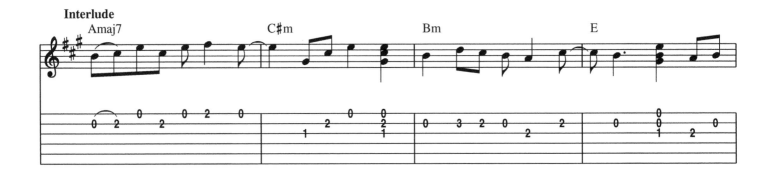

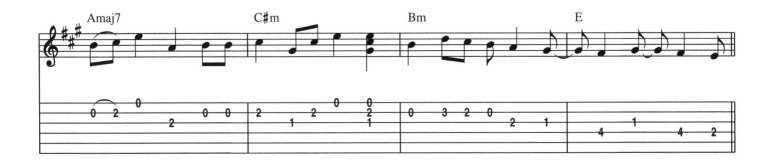

Chorus

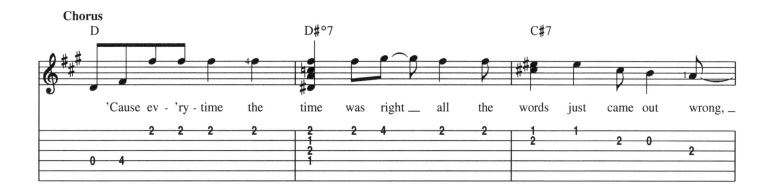

'Cause ev - 'ry - time the time was right — all the words just came out wrong, —

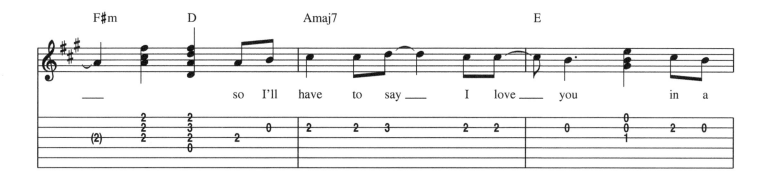

— so I'll have to say — I love — you in a

D.S. al Coda ⊕ Coda

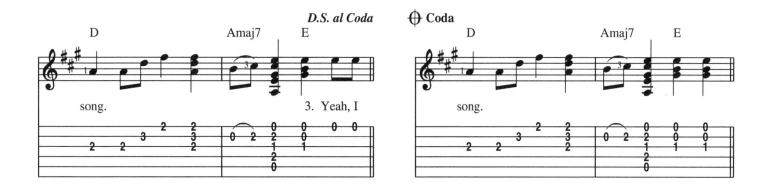

song.   3. Yeah, I   song.

Outro

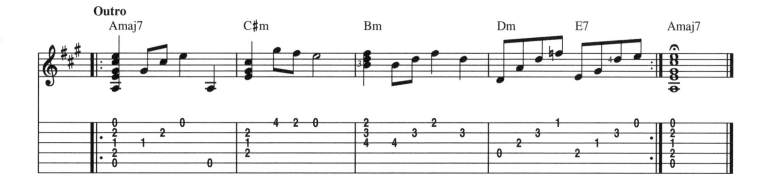

Additional Lyrics

2. Yeah, I know it's kind of strange,
   But ev'rytime I'm near you,
   I just run out of things to say
   I know you'd understand.

3. Yeah, I know it's kind of late,
   I hope I didn't wake you.
   But there's something that I just got to say
   I know you'd understand.

I Got a Name

Words by Norman Gimbel
Music by Charles Fox

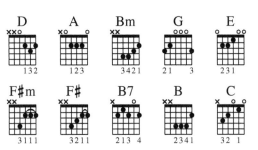

Strum Pattern: 3
Pick Pattern: 3

1. Like the pine trees
2., 3. *See additional lyrics*

lin - ing the wind - ing road, ___ I've got a name; ___

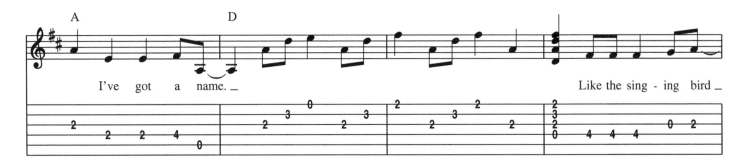

I've got a name. ___ Like the sing - ing bird ___

___ and the croak - ing toad, I've got a name; ___

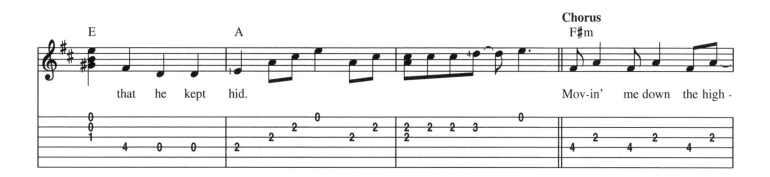

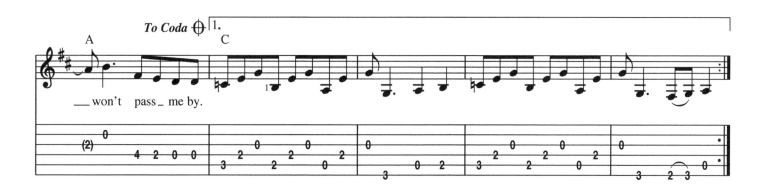

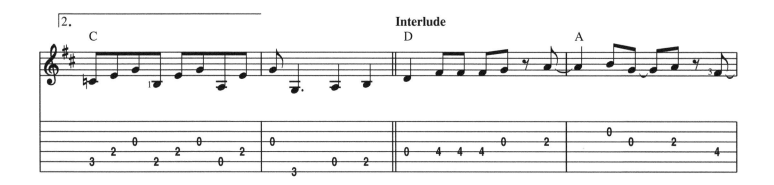

Interlude

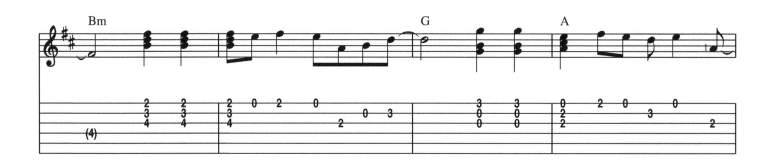

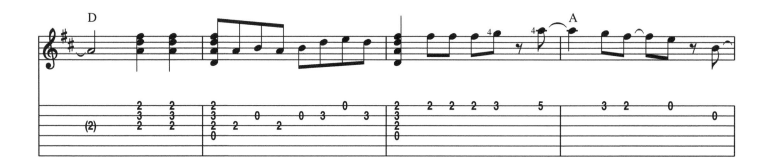

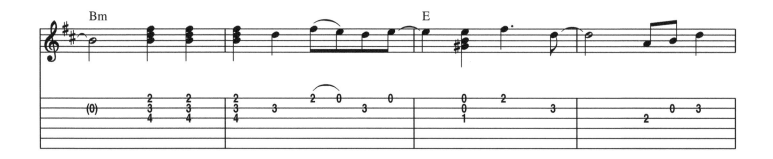

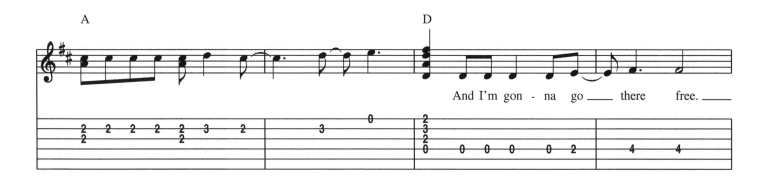

And I'm gon - na go ____ there free. ____

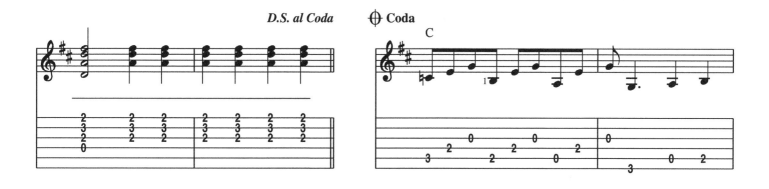

D.S. al Coda ⊕ **Coda**

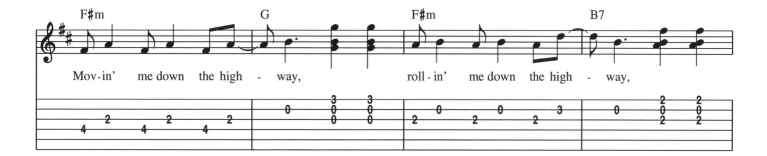

Mov-in' me down the high - way, roll-in' me down the high - way,

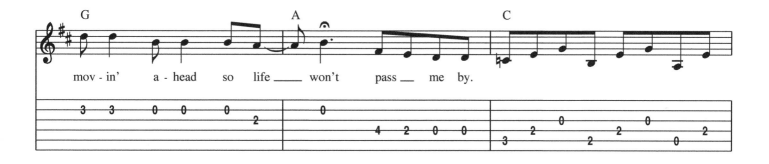

mov-in' a-head so life ____ won't pass ___ me by.

Additional Lyrics

2. Like the north wind whistlin' down the sky,
   I've got a song; I've got a song.
   Like the whip-poor-will and the baby's cry,
   I've got a song; I've got a song.
   And I carry it with me and I sing it loud;
   If it gets me nowhere,
   I'll go there proud.

3. Like the fool I am and I'll always be,
   I've got a dream; I've got a dream.
   They can change their minds but they can't change me,
   I've got a dream; I've got a dream.
   Oh, I know I could share it if you'd want me to;
   If you're goin' my way,
   I'll go with you.

Lover's Cross

Words and Music by Jim Croce

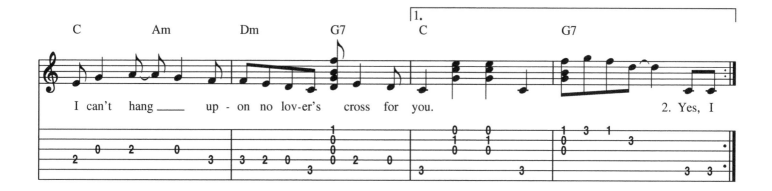

I can't hang ___ up-on no lov-er's cross for you.

2. Yes, I

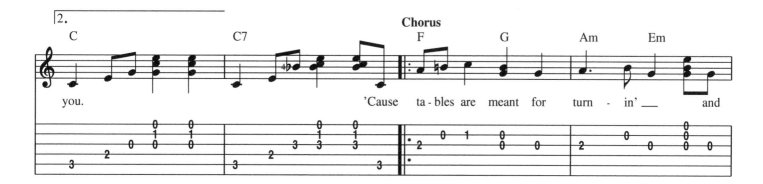

2.

Chorus

you. 'Cause ta-bles are meant for turn-in' ___ and

peo-ple are bound _ to ___ change. ___ And bridg-es are meant for burn-in' ___ when the

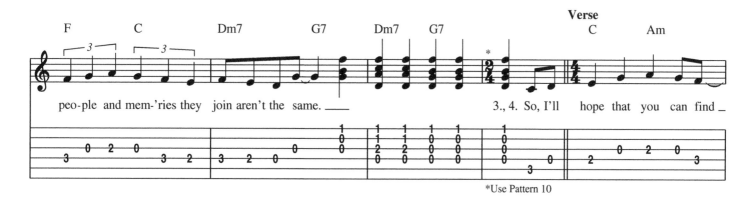

Verse

peo-ple and mem-'ries they join aren't the same. ___ 3., 4. So, I'll hope that you can find _

*Use Pattern 10

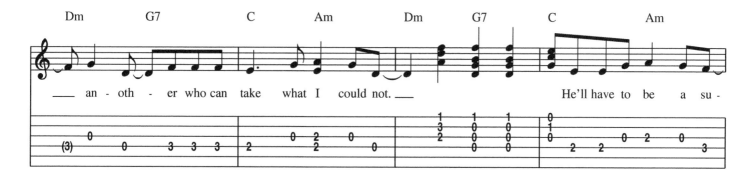

___ an - oth - er who can take what I could not. ___ He'll have to be a su-

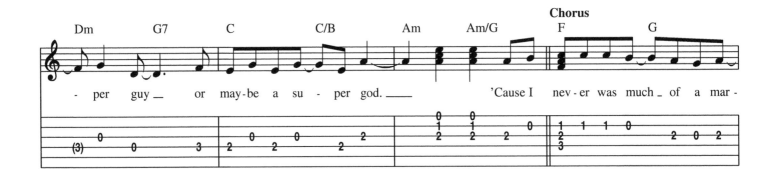

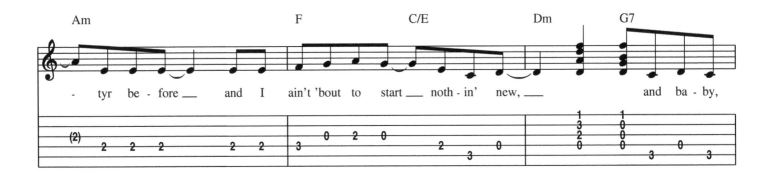

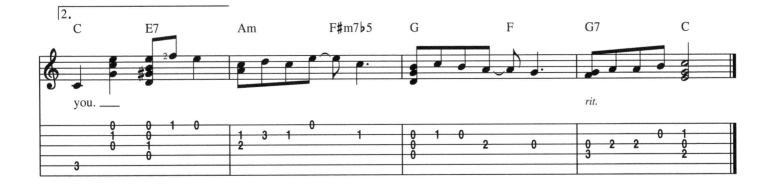

Additional Lyrics

2. Yes, I really got to hand it to you,
'Cause girl, you really tried.
But for ev'ry time that we spent laughing,
There were two times that I cried.
And you were tryin' to make me your martyr,
And that's one thing I just couldn't do,
'Cause baby, I can't hang upon no lover's cross for you.

Mississippi Lady

Words and Music by Jim Croce

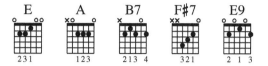

Strum Pattern: 1
Pick Pattern: 3

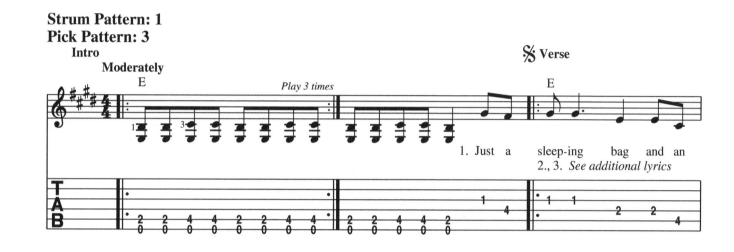

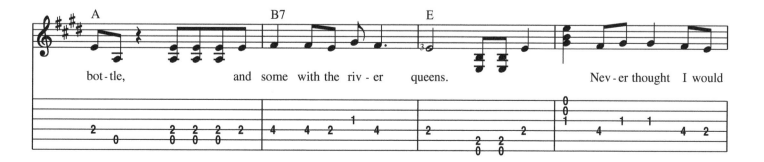

meet a girl who could turn my head __ a - round, _____ till I

met that Mis - sis - sip - pi la - dy in sleep - y Gulf - port town. __ She was __ a

Chorus

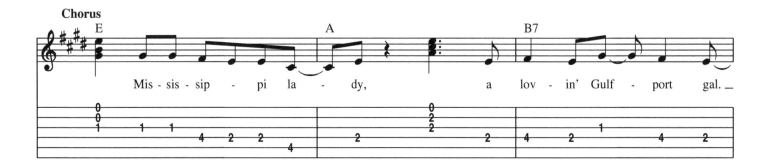

Mis - sis - sip - pi la - dy, a lov - in' Gulf - port gal.

__ She taught me how __ to love __ and she

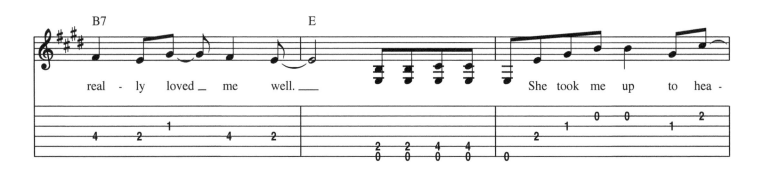

real - ly loved __ me well. __ She took me up to hea -

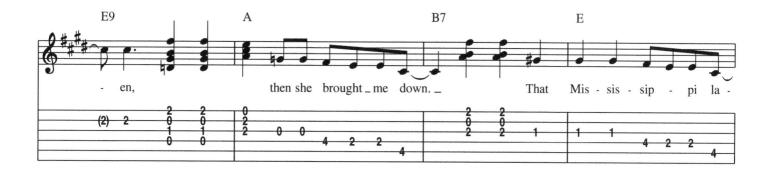

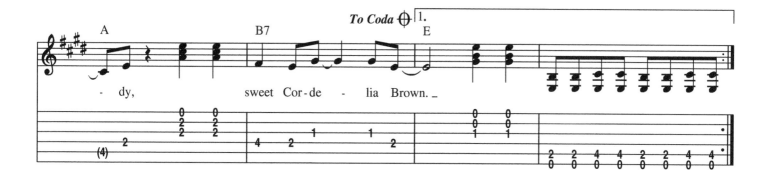

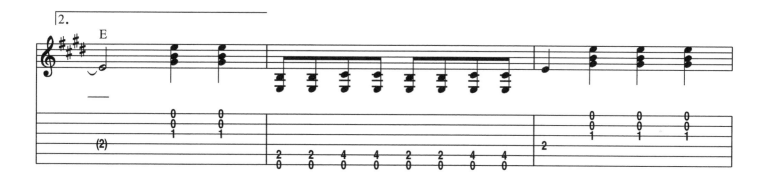

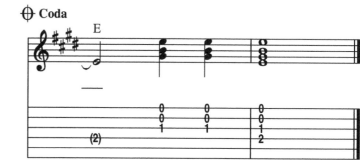

Additional Lyrics

2. Hot July in Gulfport
   And I was working in the bars.
   She was working on the street
   With the rest of the evening stars.
   She said, "I never met a guy
   Who could turn my head around."
   And that's really sayin' something,
   Sweet Cordelia Brown.

3. Now I'm back in New York City,
   Playin' in a band.
   But my mind's on Mississippi,
   Is it hard to understand?
   Never thought I would meet a girl
   Who could bring me that far down.
   Like the girl I met in Gulfport,
   Sweet Cordelia Brown.

New York's Not My Home

Words and Music by Jim Croce

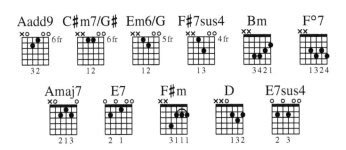

Strum Pattern: 6
Pick Pattern: 2

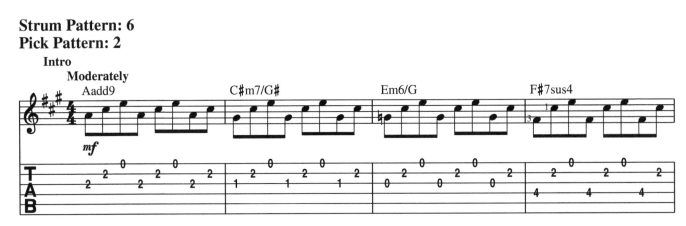

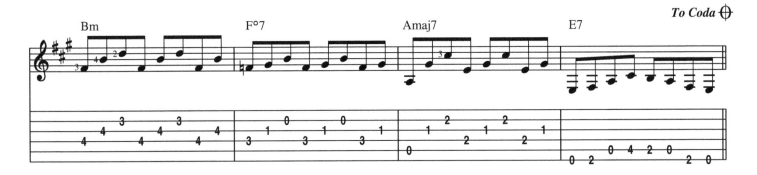

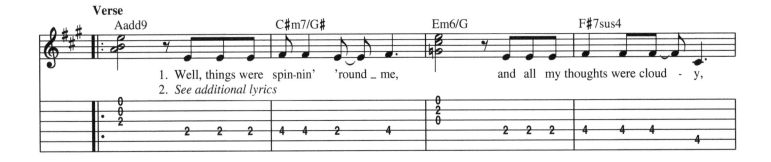

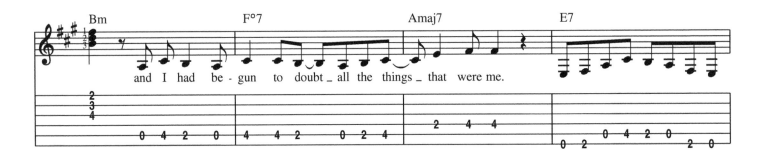

1. Well, things were spin-nin' 'round _ me, and all my thoughts were cloud - y,
2. *See additional lyrics*

and I had be - gun to doubt _ all the things _ that were me.

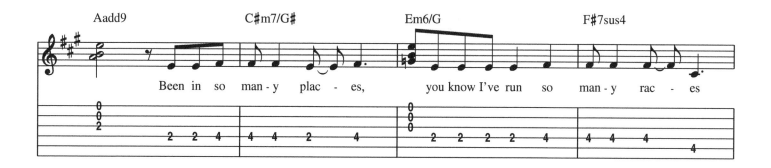

Been in so man-y plac-es, you know I've run so man-y rac-es

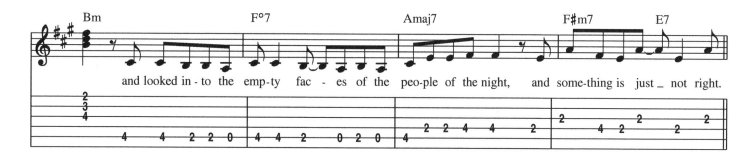

and looked in-to the emp-ty fac-es of the peo-ple of the night, and some-thing is just _ not right.

Chorus

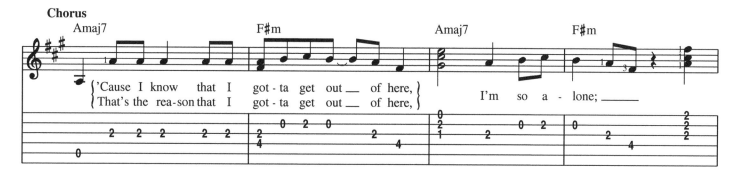

'Cause I know that I got-ta get out _ of here,
That's the rea-son that I got-ta get out _ of here,

I'm so a-lone; _____

don't you know that I got-ta get out _ of here 'cause New York's not _ my home. _

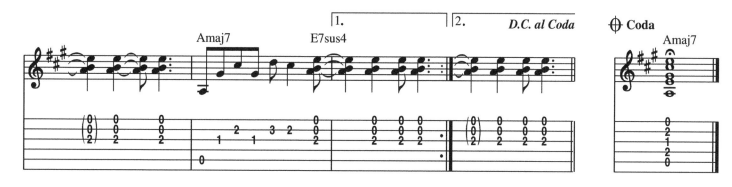

D.C. al Coda

Coda

Additional Lyrics

2. Though all the streets are crowded, there's something strange about it;
   I lived there 'bout a year and I never once felt at home.
   I thought I'd make the big time, I learned a lot of lessons awful quick and now
   I'm telling you that they were not the nice kind
   And it's been so long since I have felt fine.

One Less Set of Footsteps

Words and Music by Jim Croce

Strum Pattern: 2
Pick Pattern: 4

Intro
Moderately

Verse

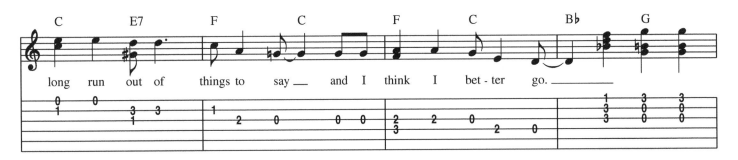

1. We been run-nin' a-way ___ from some-thin' we both know. We've

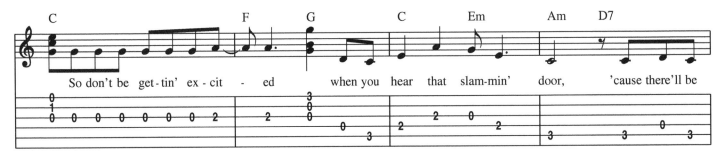

long run out of things to say ___ and I think I bet-ter go. ___

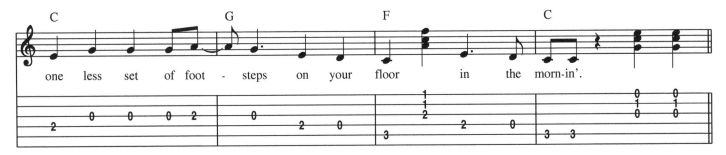

So don't be get-tin' ex-cit-ed when you hear that slam-min' door, 'cause there'll be one less set of foot-steps on your floor in the morn-in'.

Verse

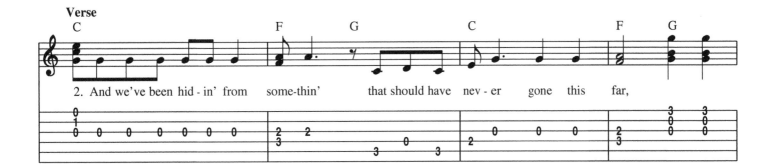

2. And we've been hid-in' from some-thin' that should have nev-er gone this far,

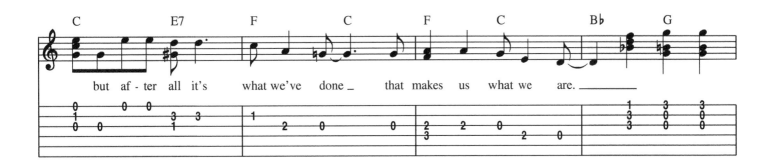

but af-ter all it's what we've done _ that makes us what we are. _____

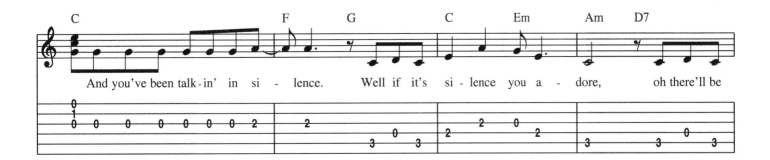

And you've been talk-in' in si - lence. Well if it's si - lence you a - dore, oh there'll be

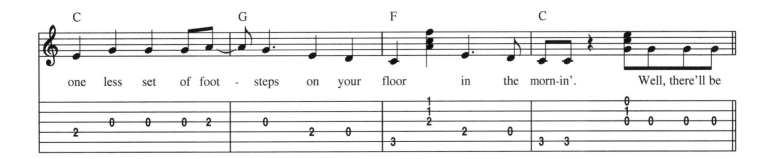

one less set of foot - steps on your floor in the morn-in'. Well, there'll be

Bridge

one less set of foot - steps on your floor, one less man to walk _ in.

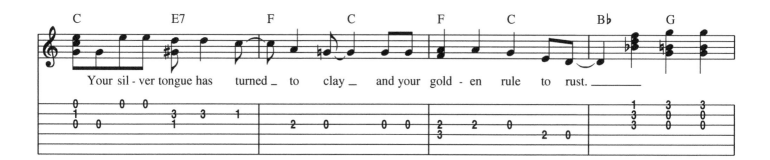

Outro

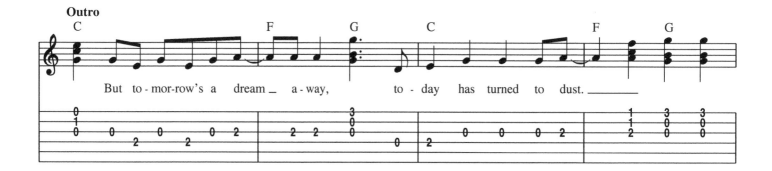

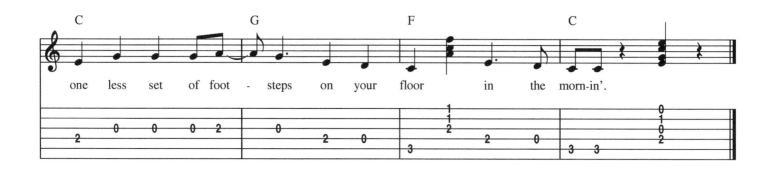

Operator
(That's Not the Way It Feels)

Words and Music by Jim Croce

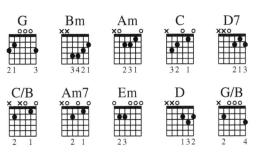

Strum Pattern: 4
Pick Pattern: 6

Intro
Moderately

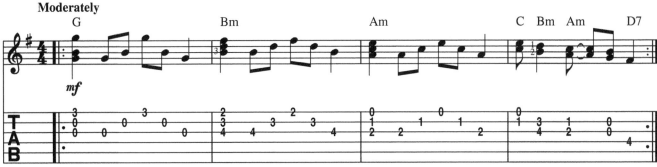

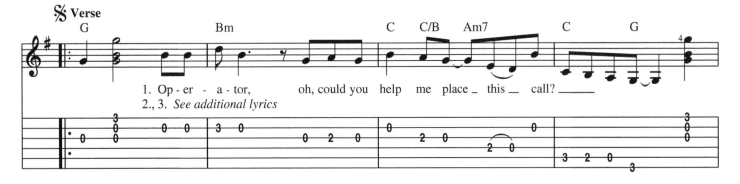

1. Op - er - a - tor, oh, could you help me place _ this _ call? _____
2., 3. *See additional lyrics*

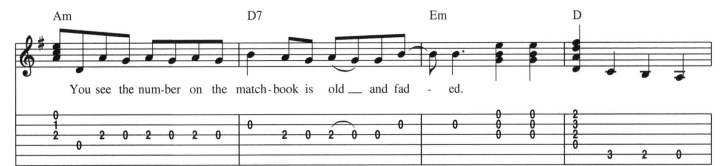

You see the num - ber on the match - book is old _ and fad - ed.

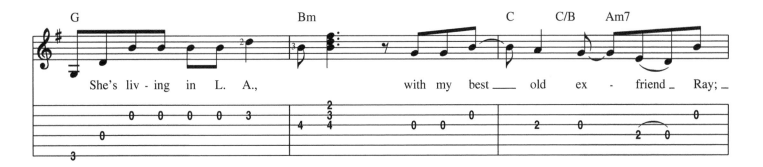

She's liv - ing in L. A., with my best _ old ex - friend _ Ray; _

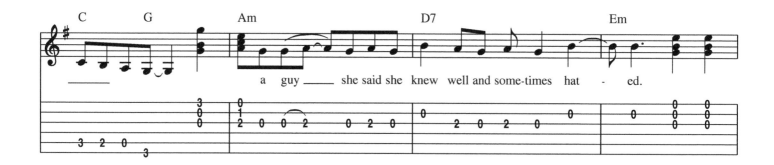

a guy ___ she said she knew well and some-times hat - ed.

Chorus

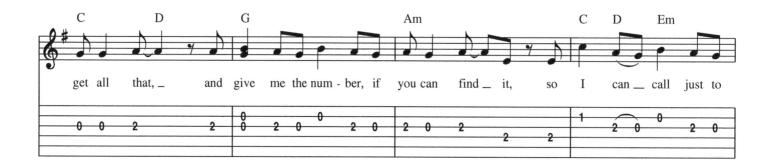

Is - n't that the way ___ they ___ say it goes? But let's for -

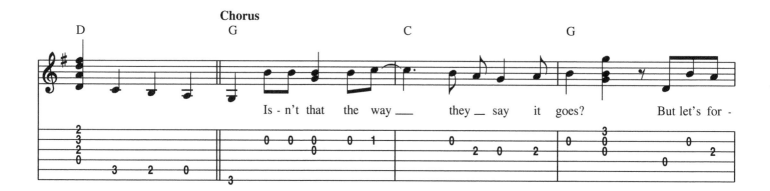

get all that, _ and give me the num - ber, if you can find _ it, so I can _ call just to

tell them I'm fine and to show ___ I've o - ver-come the blow, I've learned to take it well, _

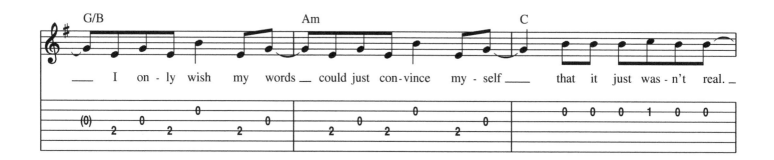

___ I on - ly wish my words _ could just con - vince my - self ___ that it just was - n't real.

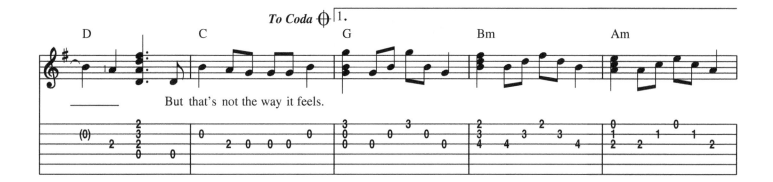

To Coda ⊕ |1.

But that's not the way it feels.

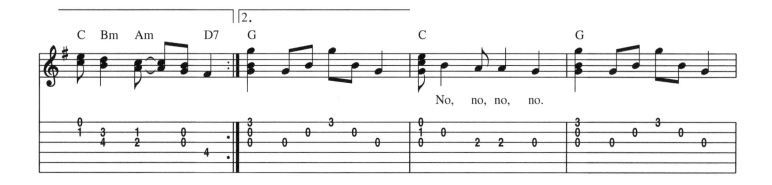

|2.

No, no, no, no.

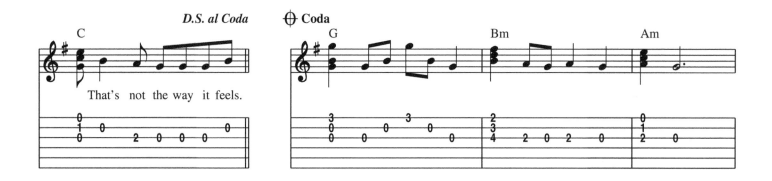

D.S. al Coda   ⊕ *Coda*

That's not the way it feels.

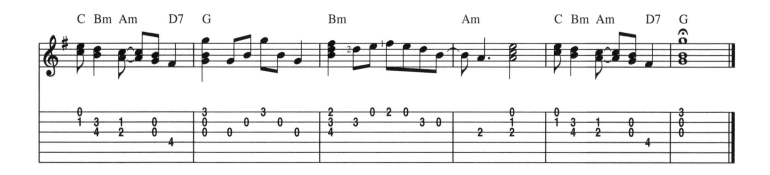

Additional Lyrics

2. Operator, oh, could you help me place this call?
   'Cause I can't read the number that you just gave me.
   There's something in my eyes.
   You know it happens everytime
   I think about the love that I thought would save me.

3. Operator, oh, let's forget about this call.
   (There's) no one there I really wanted to talk to.
   Thank you for your time.
   Oh, you've been so much more than kind,
   You can keep the dime.

Photographs and Memories

Words and Music by Jim Croce

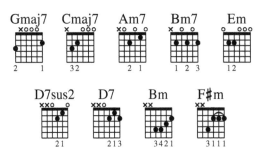

Gmaj7   Cmaj7   Am7   Bm7   Em

D7sus2   D7   Bm   F#m

Strum Pattern: 5
Pick Pattern: 2, 4

Intro
Moderately

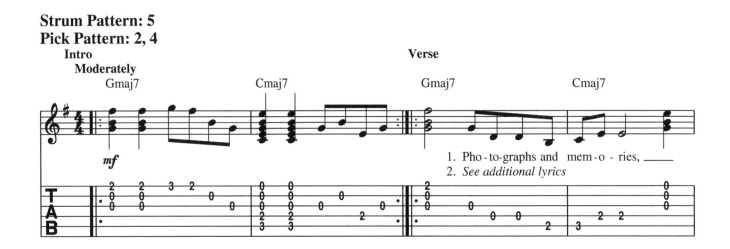

1. Pho-to-graphs and mem-o-ries, _____
2. *See additional lyrics*

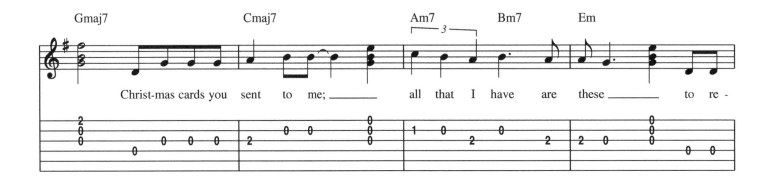

Christ-mas cards you sent to me; _____ all that I have are these _____ to re-

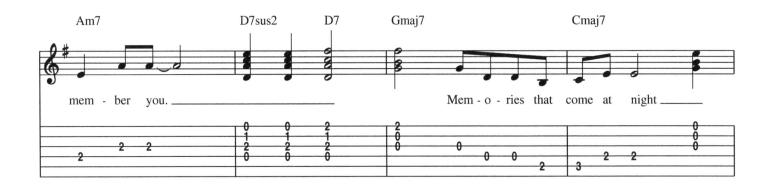

mem - ber you. _____ Mem - o - ries that come at night _____

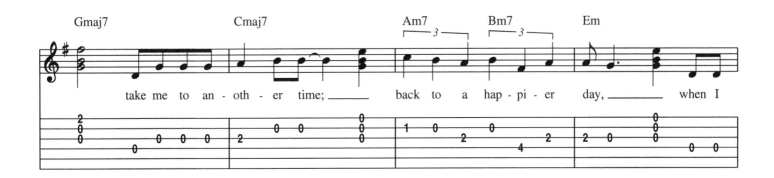

take me to an-oth-er time; ____ back to a hap-pi-er day, ____ when I

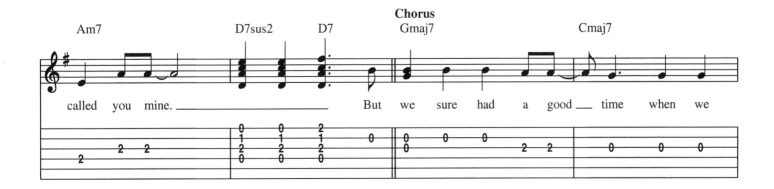

Chorus

called you mine. _____ But we sure had a good __ time when we

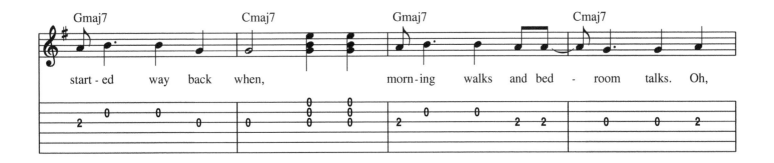

start-ed way back when, morn-ing walks and bed-room talks. Oh,

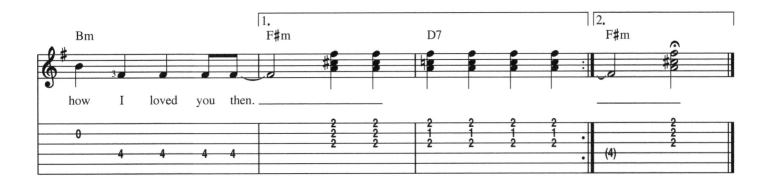

how I loved you then. _____

Additional Lyrics

2. Summer skies and lullabies, nights we couldn't say good-bye;
   And of all of the things that we knew not a dream survived.
   Photographs and memories, all the love you gave to me;
   Somehow it just can't be true. That's all I've left of you.

Rapid Roy
(The Stock Car Boy)

Words and Music by Jim Croce

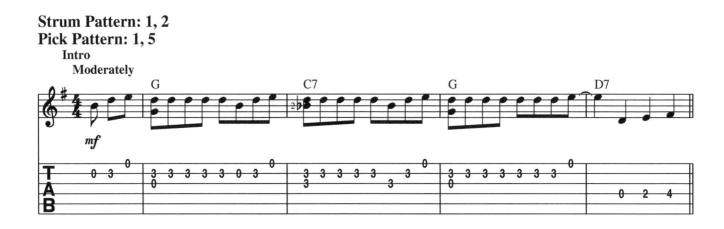

Strum Pattern: 1, 2
Pick Pattern: 1, 5

Intro
Moderately

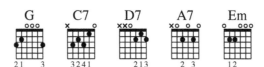

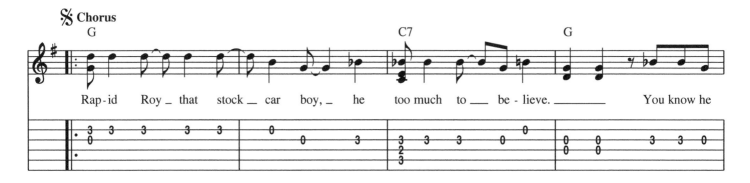

Rap-id Roy _ that stock _ car boy, _ he too much to __ be - lieve. _____ You know he

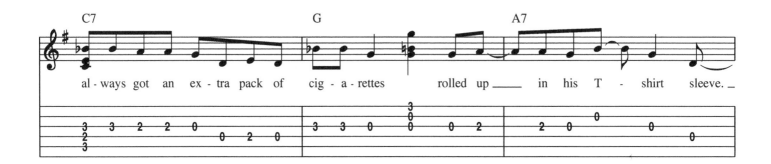

al - ways got an ex - tra pack of cig - a - rettes rolled up ___ in his T - shirt sleeve.

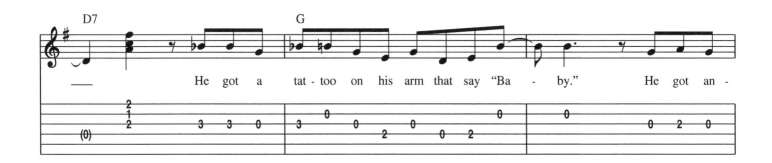

___ He got a tat - too on his arm that say "Ba - by." He got an -

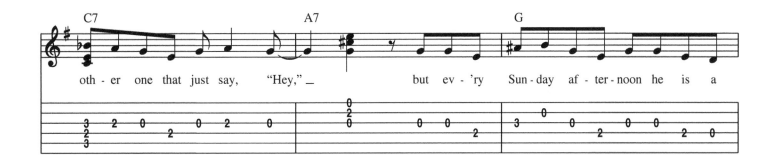

oth - er one that just say, "Hey," _ but ev - 'ry Sun - day af - ter - noon he is a

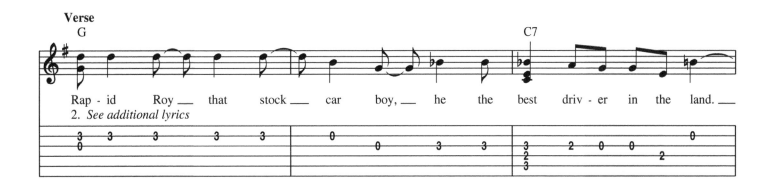

To Coda ⊕

dirt track de - mon in a Fif - ty - sev - en Chev - ro - let. _____ 1. Oh,

Verse

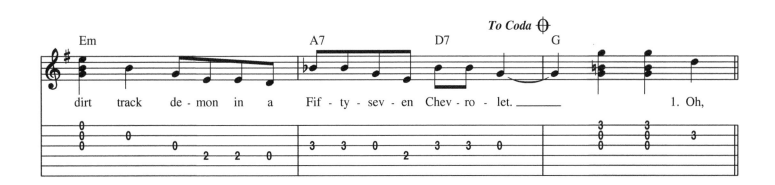

Rap - id Roy _ that stock _ car boy, _ he the best driv - er in the land. _
2. See additional lyrics

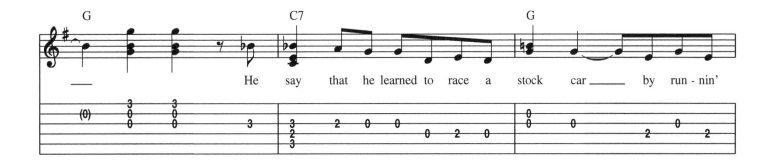

He say that he learned to race a stock car _ by run - nin'

'shine out - a Al - a - bam'. _____ Oh the Dem - o - li - tion Der - by and the

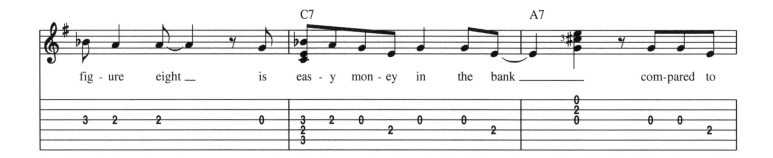

fig - ure eight __ is eas - y mon - ey in the bank _____ com - pared to

run - nin' from the man in ____ O - kla - ho - ma Cit - y with a five hun - dred gal - lon tank. __

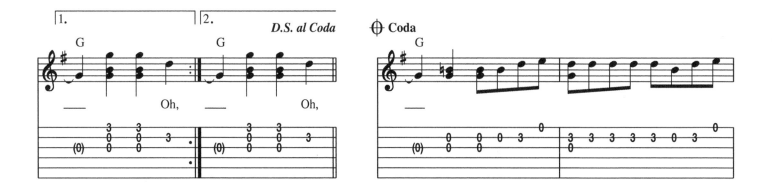

__ Oh, __ Oh,

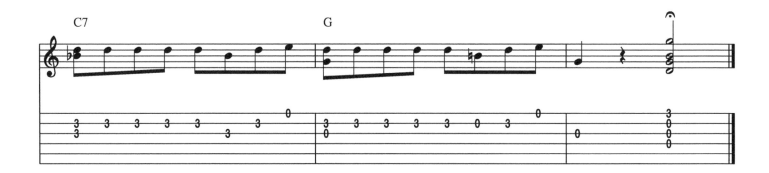

Additional Lyrics

2. Oh Roy so cool, that racin' fool,
   He don't know what fear's about;
   He do a hundred thirty mile an hour, smilin' at the cam'ra,
   With a toothpick in his mouth.
   He got a girl back home, name of Dixie Dawn,
   But he got honeys all along the way;
   And you oughta hear them screamin' for that dirt track demon
   In a Fifty-seven Chevrolet.

Roller Derby Queen

Words and Music by Jim Croce

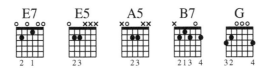

Strum Pattern: 1
Pick Pattern: 3

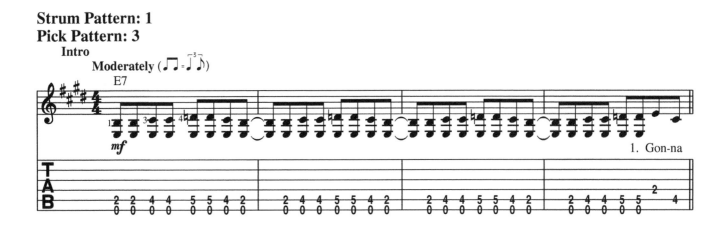

43

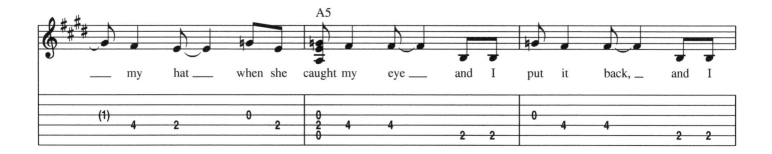

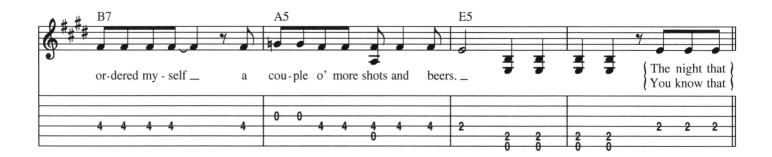

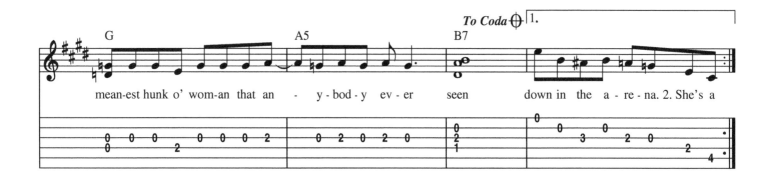

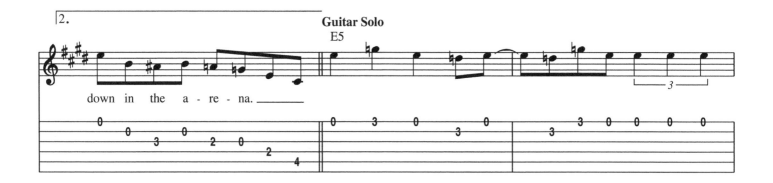

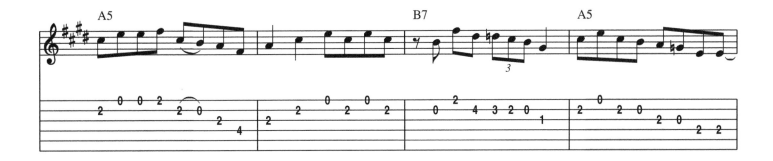

D.S. al Coda   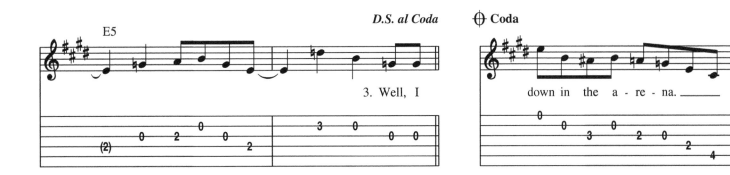 **Coda**

3. Well, I

down in the a - re - na. _____

Outro

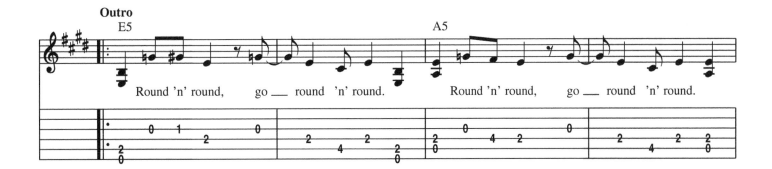

Round 'n' round,   go _ round 'n' round.   Round 'n' round,   go _ round 'n' round.

Repeat and fade

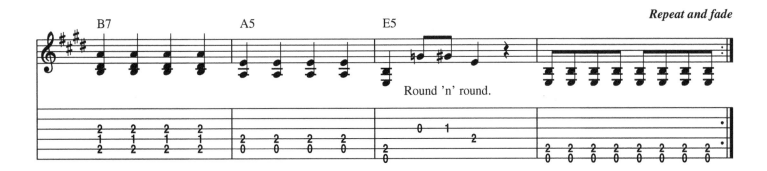

Round 'n' round.

Additional Lyrics

2. She's a five foot six and two fifteen,
   A bleached blonde mama with a streak of mean;
   She knew how to knuckle and knew how to scuffle and fight,
   And the Roller Derby program said
   That she were built like a 'frigerator with a head;
   The fans called her "Tuffy," but all her buddies called her "Spike."

3. Well, I could not help but fall in love
   With this heavy duty woman I been speakin' of;
   Things looked kind of bad until the day she skated into my life.
   Well, she might be nasty, she might be fat,
   But I never met a person who would tell her that;
   She's my big blonde bomber, my heavy handed Hackensack Mama.

Spin, Spin, Spin

Words and Music by Jim Croce and Ingrid Croce

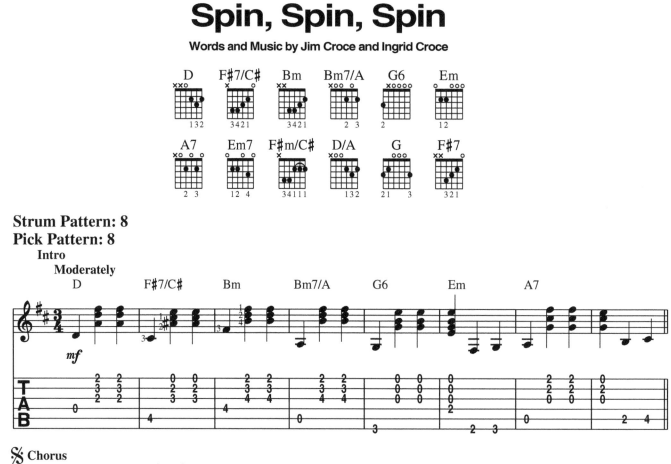

Strum Pattern: 8
Pick Pattern: 8

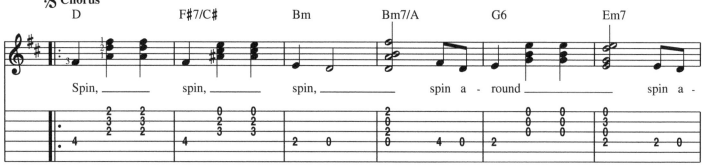

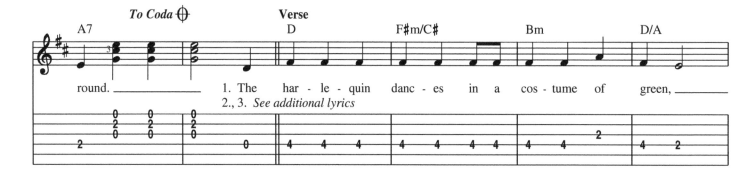

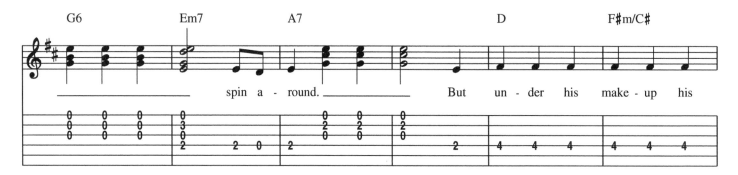

46

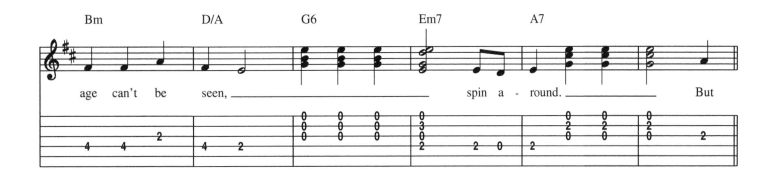

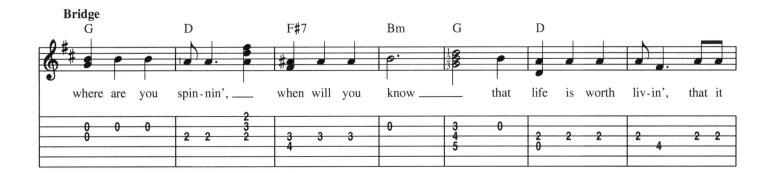

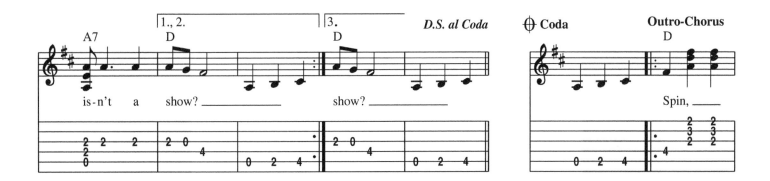

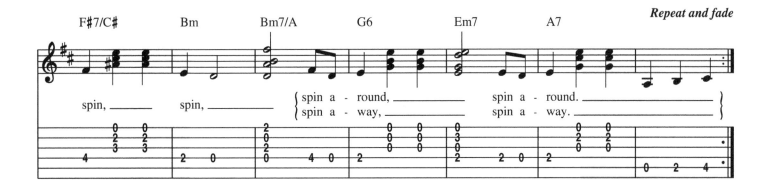

Additional Lyrics

2. You look out on the city from your penthouse so high,
   Spin around.
   But your pedestal's your prison and so is your high,
   Spin around.

3. Your pills are your conscience, they make ev'rything seem all right,
   Spin around.
   Take a white one to go to sleep, take a red one to stay up all night
   To spin around.

These Dreams

Words and Music by Jim Croce

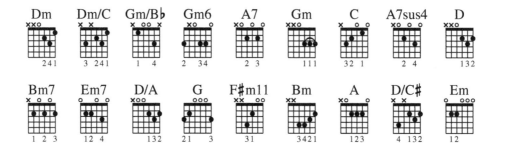

Strum Pattern: 3
Pick Pattern: 2

Intro
Moderately

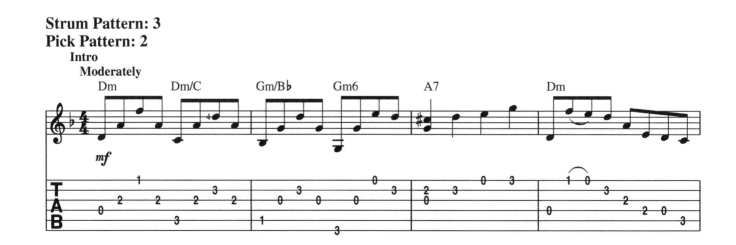

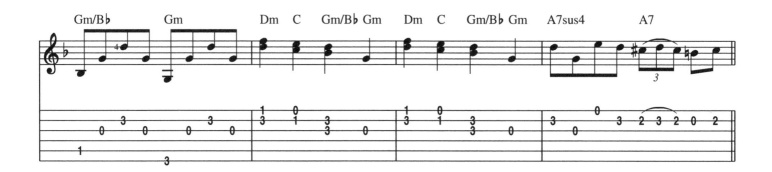

Verse

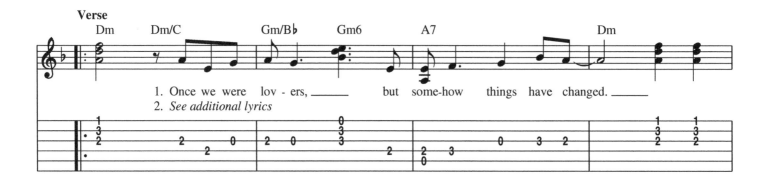

1. Once we were lov-ers, _____ but some-how things have changed. _____
2. *See additional lyrics*

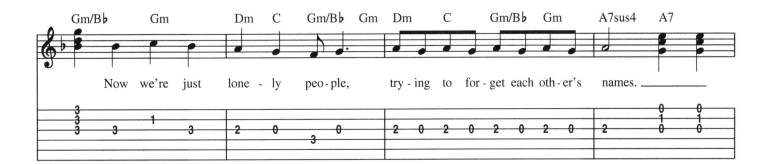

Now we're just lone - ly peo - ple, try - ing to for - get each oth - er's names. _____

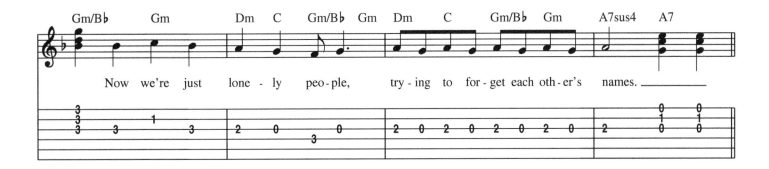

Now we're just lone - ly peo - ple, try - ing to for - get each oth - er's names. _____

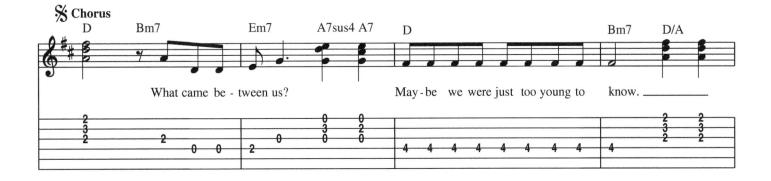

%% **Chorus**

What came be - tween us? May - be we were just too young to know. _____

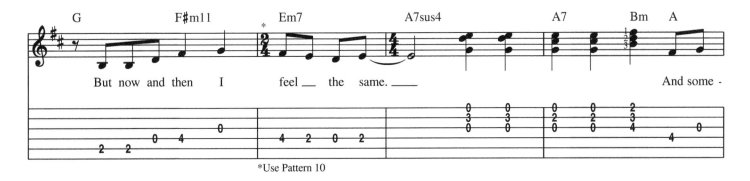

But now and then I feel __ the same. __ And some -

*Use Pattern 10

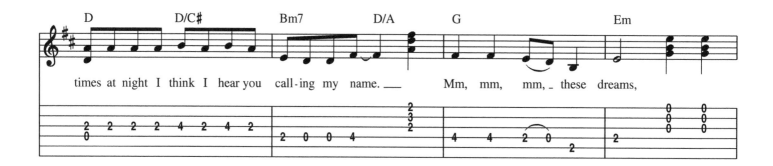

times at night I think I hear you call-ing my name. ___ Mm, mm, mm, __ these dreams,

they keep me go-in' these days. _____

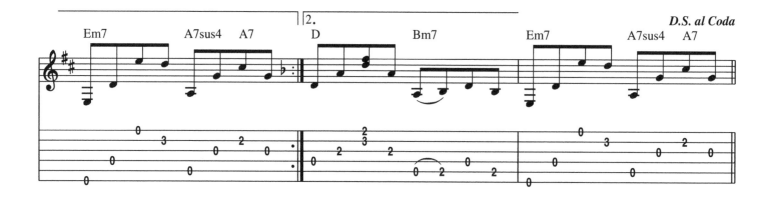

Additional Lyrics

2. Once we were lovers, but that was long ago.
   We lived together then and now we do not even say hello.
   We lived together then and now we do not even say hello.

Vespers

Words and Music by Jim Croce and Ingrid Croce

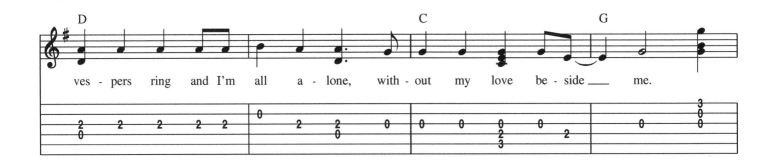

ves - pers ring and I'm all a - lone, with - out my love be - side ____ me.

%̸ Verse
G

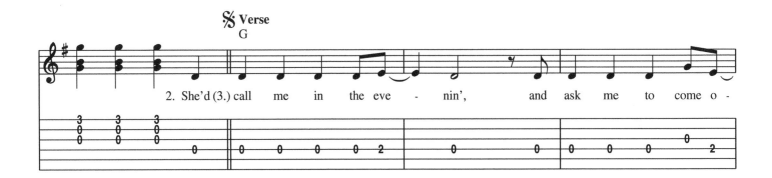

2. She'd (3.) call me in the eve - nin', and ask me to come o -

- ver, she'd be stand - ing by the win - dow with her hair down a - round her shoul -

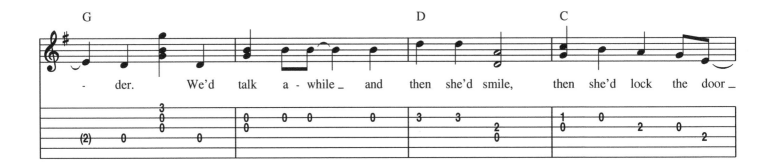

- der. We'd talk a - while __ and then she'd smile, then she'd lock the door __

To Coda ⊕

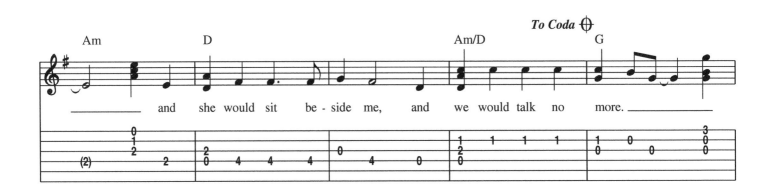

____ and she would sit be - side me, and we would talk no more. ____

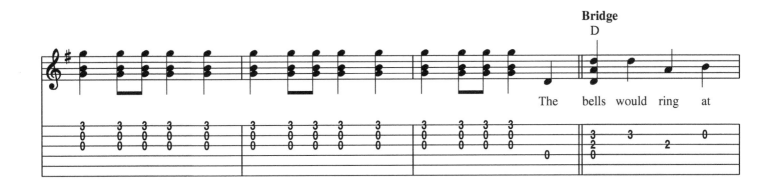

Bridge

The bells would ring at

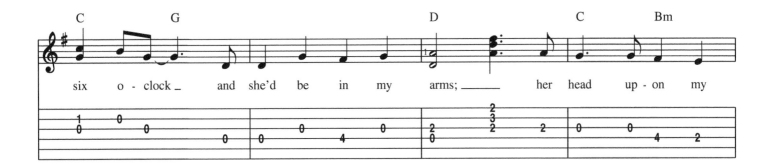

six o-clock _ and she'd be in my arms; _____ her head up-on my

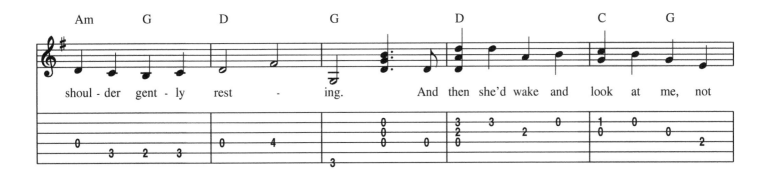

shoul-der gent-ly rest - ing. And then she'd wake and look at me, not

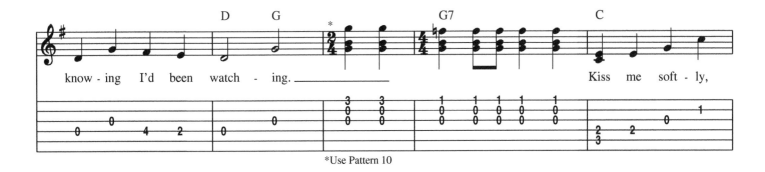

know-ing I'd been watch-ing. _____ Kiss me soft-ly,

*Use Pattern 10

D.S. al Coda ⊕ **Coda**

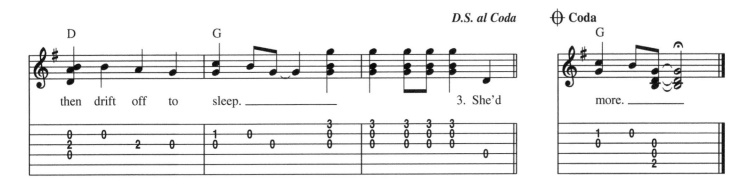

then drift off to sleep. _____ 3. She'd   more. _____

Time in a Bottle

Words and Music by Jim Croce

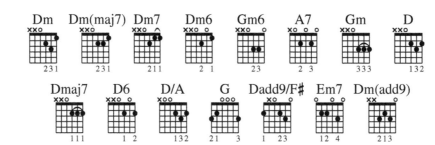

Strum Pattern: 9
Pick Pattern: 9

Intro
Moderately

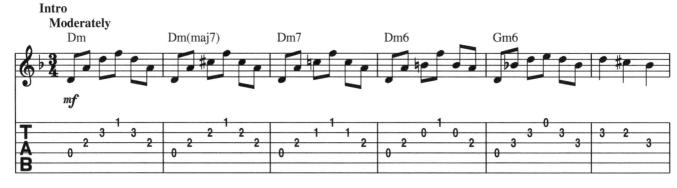

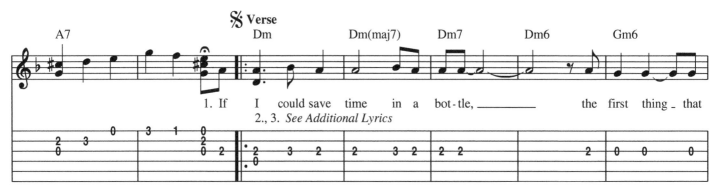

1. If I could save time in a bot-tle, _____ the first thing _ that
2., 3. *See Additional Lyrics*

I'd like to do. _____ is to save ev-'ry day till e-ter-ni-ty pass-es a-way just to

spend them with you. _____ 2. If ___ But there nev-er seems _ to be e-nough time _ to

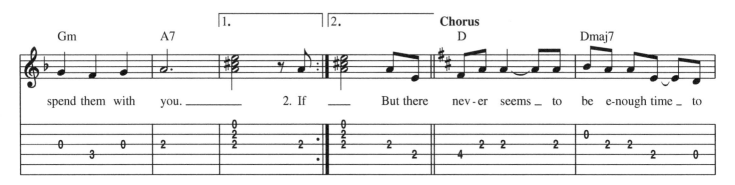

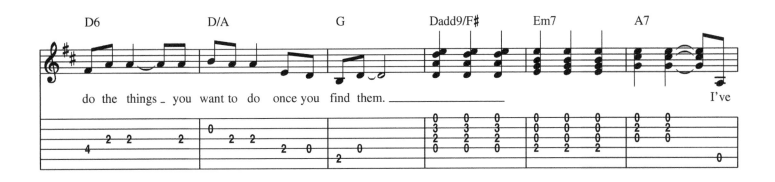

do the things _ you want to do   once you find them. _____ I've

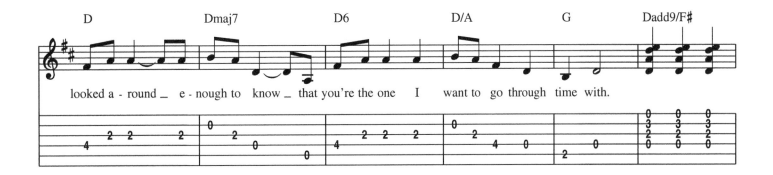

looked a - round _ e - nough to   know _ that you're the one   I   want to go through   time with.

Interlude
To Coda ⊕

D.S. al Coda
(take 2nd ending)

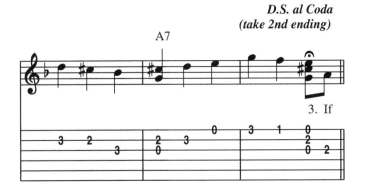

3. If

⊕ *Coda*
Outro

Additional Lyrics

2. If I could make days last forever,
   If words could make wishes come true,
   I'd save ev'ry day like a treasure, and then
   Again I would spend them with you.

3. If I had a box just for wishes,
   And dreams that had never come true,
   The box would be empty except for the mem'ry
   Of how they were answered by you.

Walkin' Back to Georgia

Words and Music by Jim Croce

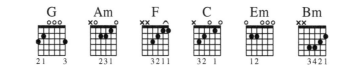

Strum Pattern: 1, 3
Pick Pattern: 2, 4

Intro
Moderately

Hmm, _____ hmm, _____ hmm.

Verse

1. I'm walk-in' back to Geor - gia, and I hope she will take me _ back; _____
2. *See additional lyrics*

noth-in' in my pock-ets, _____ and all I own is up-on my _ back. _ 1., 2. But she's the

Chorus

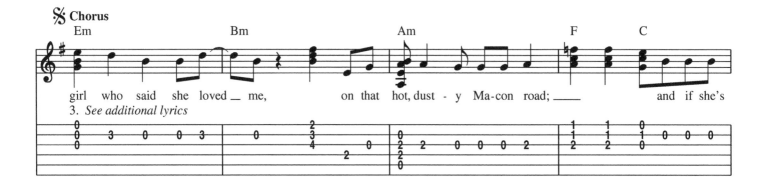

girl who said she loved _ me, on that hot, dust - y Ma-con road; _____ and if she's
3. *See additional lyrics*

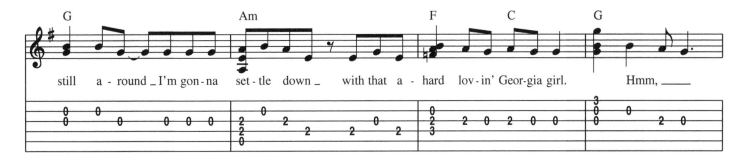

still a-round _ I'm gon-na set-tle down _ with that a - hard lov-in' Geor-gia girl. Hmm, _____

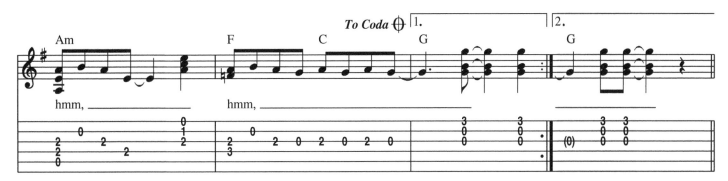

hmm, _____ hmm, _____

Verse

3. Geor-gia, can't you hear me call - in', _____ I'll be home in ____ just a while, _

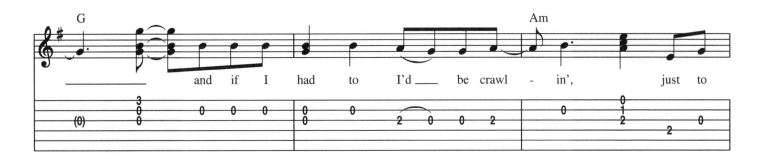

_____ and if I had to I'd ____ be crawl - in', just to

D.S. al Coda ⊕ **Coda**

share an - oth - er morn - in' ____ smile. _ But you're the _____

Additional Lyrics

2. I'm walkin' back to Georgia,
She's the only one who knows
How it feels when you lose a dream;
How it feels when you dream alone.

Chorus 3. But you're the girl who said you loved me,
On that hot, dusty long ago;
And if you're still around,
I'm gonna settle down
With you, my hard lovin' Georgia girl.
Hmm, hmm, hmm.

Workin' at the Car Wash Blues

Words and Music by Jim Croce

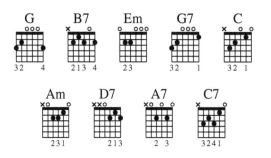

Strum Pattern: 3, 6
Pick Pattern: 1, 3

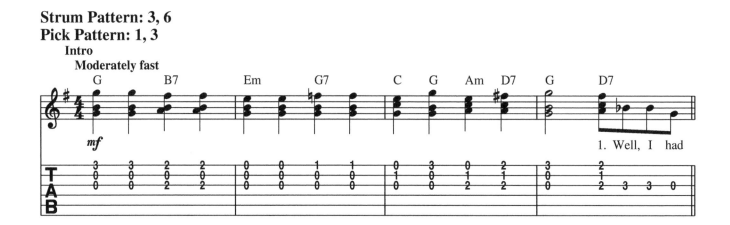

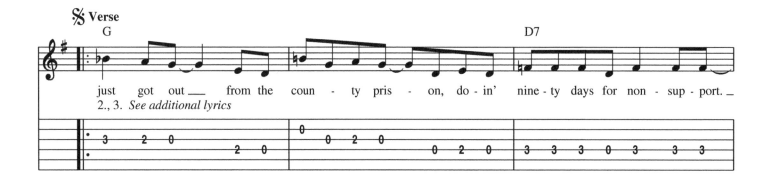

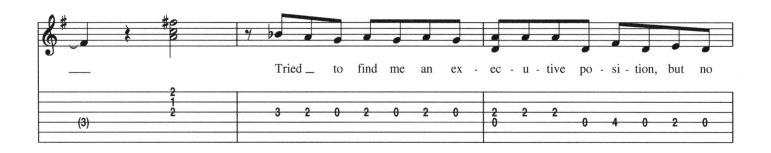

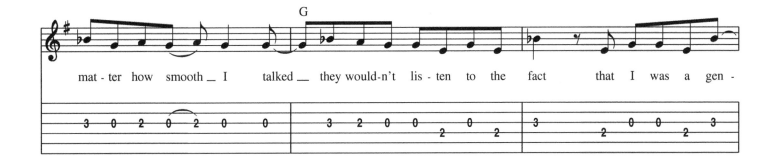

mat - ter how smooth _ I talked _ they would-n't lis - ten to the fact that I was a gen -

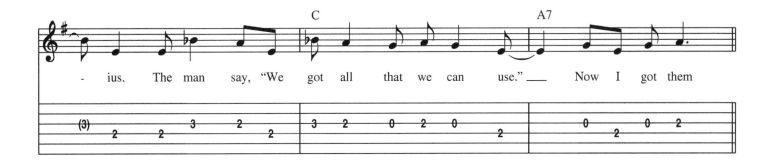

- ius. The man say, "We got all that we can use." __ Now I got them

Chorus

To Coda ⊕

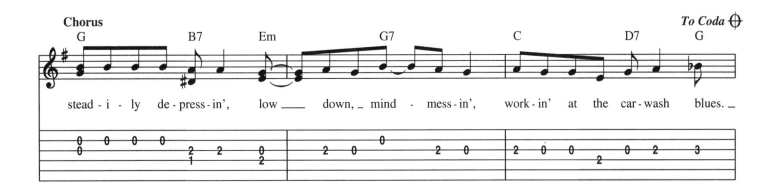

stead - i - ly de - press - in', low __ down, _ mind - mess - in', work - in' at the car - wash blues. __

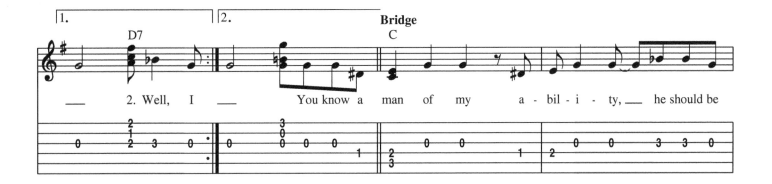

2. Well, I __ You know a man of my a - bil - i - ty, __ he should be

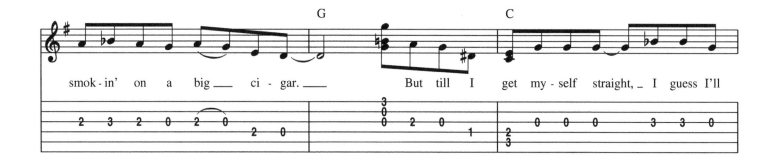

smok-in' on a big __ ci - gar. ____ But till I get my-self straight, _ I guess I'll

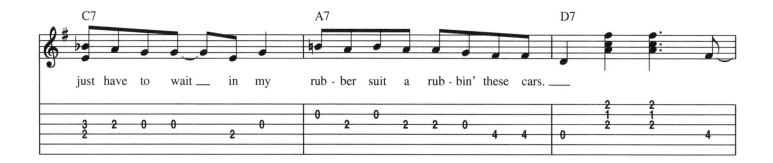

just have to wait __ in my rub - ber suit a rub-bin' these cars. ____

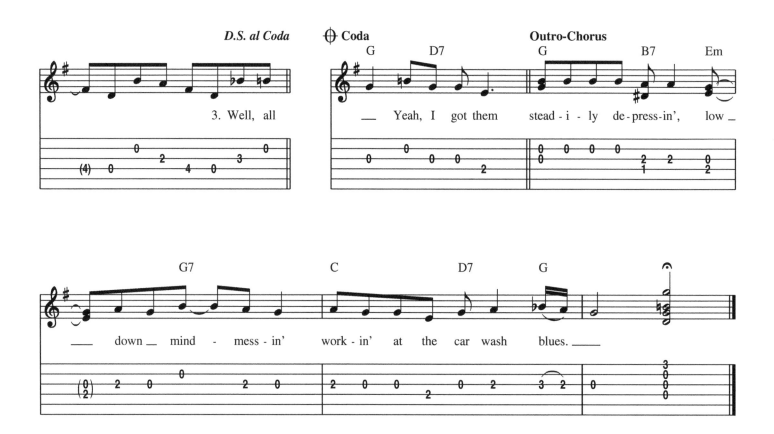

D.S. al Coda   Coda   **Outro-Chorus**

3. Well, all   ___ Yeah, I got them stead-i-ly de-press-in', low _

___ down __ mind - mess-in' work-in' at the car wash blues. ____

Additional Lyrics

2. Well, I should be sittin' in an air-conditioned office in a swivel chair,
   Talkin' some trash to the secretaries, sayin' "Here now, mama, come over here."
   Instead, I'm stuck here rubbin' these fenders with a rag
   And walkin' home in soggy old shoes with them...

3. Well, all I can do is a shake my head, you might not believe it's true,
   For workin' at this end of Niagara Falls is an undiscovered Howard Hughes.
   So, baby, don't expect to see me with no double martini
   In any high-brow society news, 'cause I got them...

You Don't Mess Around With Jim

Words and Music by Jim Croce

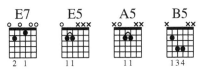

Strum Pattern: 4
Pick Pattern: 1

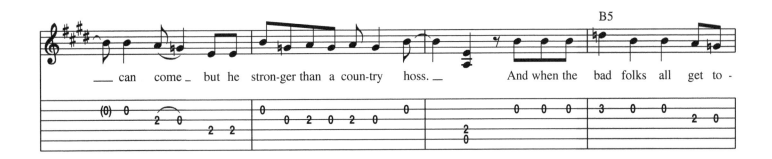

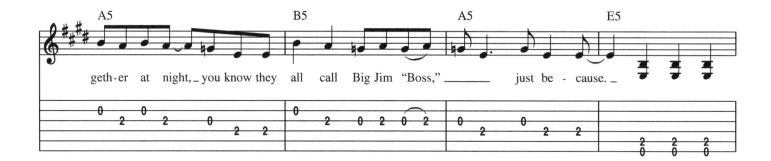

geth-er at night, _ you know they all call Big Jim "Boss," _____ just be - cause. _

Chorus
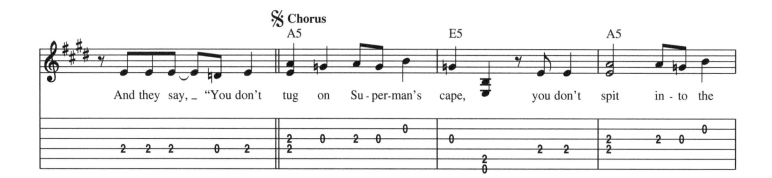

And they say, _ "You don't tug on Su - per-man's cape, you don't spit in - to the

To Coda
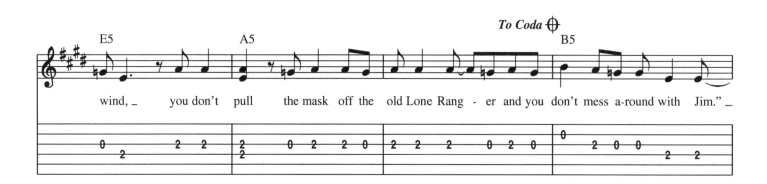

wind, _ you don't pull the mask off the old Lone Rang - er and you don't mess a-round with Jim." _

1., 2.

__ Ba, da, da, la, la, di, di, di, di, di, di. ___ 2. Well, out - a

3.

Bridge
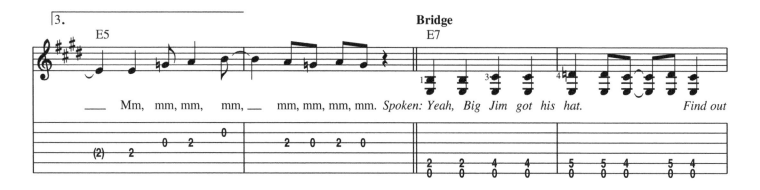

__ Mm, mm, mm, mm, __ mm, mm, mm, mm. *Spoken: Yeah, Big Jim got his hat.* *Find out*

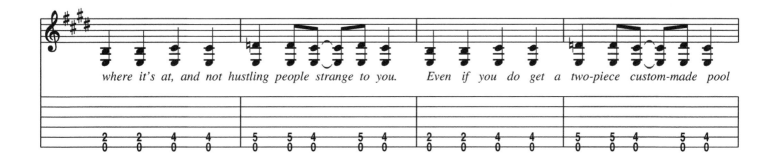

where it's at, and not hustling people strange to you. *Even if you do get a two-piece custom-made pool*

D.S. al Coda ϕ **Coda**

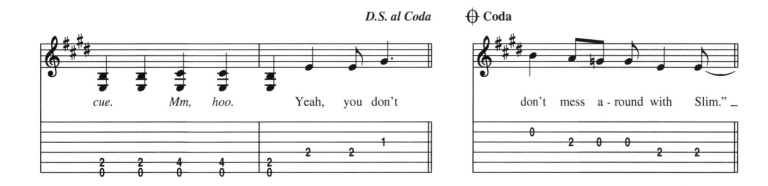

cue.   *Mm,*   *hoo.*   Yeah,   you don't   don't   mess a - round with   Slim." _

E5   ***Repeat and fade***

_ Mm, mm, mm,   mm, _ mm, mm, mm, mm,   mm. Mm, mm,   mm. _

Additional Lyrics

2. Well, outa South Alabama come a country boy.
   He said, "I'm lookin' for a man named Jim,
   I am a pool shootin' boy, my name is Willie McCoy
   But down home they call me Slim.
   Yeah, I'm lookin' for the King of Forty-second Street,
   He drivin' a drop-top Cadillac.
   Last week, he took all my money and it may sound funny,
   But I come to get my money back."
   And ev'rybody say, "Jack, Oo! Don't you know that you don't...

3. Well, a hush fell over the pool room,
   Jimmy come boppin' in off the street.
   And when the cuttin' were done the only part that wasn't bloody
   Was the soles of the big man's feet.
   Yeah, he were cut in 'bout a hundred places
   And he were shot in a couple more.
   And you better believe they sung a diff'rent kind of story
   When a Big Jim hit the floor.
   Oh, now they say you don't...

EASY GUITAR WITH NOTES & TAB

This series features simplified arrangements with notes, tab, chord charts, and strum and pick patterns.

MIXED FOLIOS

00702287	Acoustic	$19.99
00702002	Acoustic Rock Hits for Easy Guitar	$17.99
00702166	All-Time Best Guitar Collection	$29.99
00702232	Best Acoustic Songs for Easy Guitar	$16.99
00119835	Best Children's Songs	$16.99
00703055	The Big Book of Nursery Rhymes & Children's Songs	$16.99
00698978	Big Christmas Collection	$19.99
00702394	Bluegrass Songs for Easy Guitar	$15.99
00289632	Bohemian Rhapsody	$19.99
00703387	Celtic Classics	$16.99
00224808	Chart Hits of 2016-2017	$14.99
00267383	Chart Hits of 2017-2018	$14.99
00334293	Chart Hits of 2019-2020	$16.99
00403479	Chart Hits of 2021-2022	$16.99
00702149	Children's Christian Songbook	$9.99
00702028	Christmas Classics	$9.99
00101779	Christmas Guitar	$16.99
00702141	Classic Rock	$8.95
00159642	Classical Melodies	$12.99
00253933	Disney/Pixar's Coco	$19.99
00702203	CMT's 100 Greatest Country Songs	$34.99
00702283	The Contemporary Christian Collection	$16.99
00196954	Contemporary Disney	$19.99
00702239	Country Classics for Easy Guitar	$24.99
00702257	Easy Acoustic Guitar Songs	$17.99
00702041	Favorite Hymns for Easy Guitar	$12.99
00222701	Folk Pop Songs	$19.99
00126894	Frozen	$14.99
00333922	Frozen 2	$14.99
00702286	Glee	$16.99
00702160	The Great American Country Songbook	$19.99
00702148	Great American Gospel for Guitar	$14.99
00702050	Great Classical Themes for Easy Guitar	$9.99
00148030	Halloween Guitar Songs	$17.99
00702273	Irish Songs	$14.99
00192503	Jazz Classics for Easy Guitar	$16.99
00702275	Jazz Favorites for Easy Guitar	$17.99
00702274	Jazz Standards for Easy Guitar	$19.99
00702162	Jumbo Easy Guitar Songbook	$24.99
00232285	La La Land	$16.99
00702258	Legends of Rock	$14.99
00702189	MTV's 100 Greatest Pop Songs	$34.99
00702272	1950s Rock	$16.99
00702271	1960s Rock	$16.99
00702270	1970s Rock	$24.99
00702269	1980s Rock	$16.99
00702268	1990s Rock	$24.99
00369043	Rock Songs for Kids	$14.99
00109725	Once	$14.99
00702187	Selections from O Brother Where Art Thou?	$19.99
00702178	100 Songs for Kids	$16.99
00702515	Pirates of the Caribbean	$17.99
00702125	Praise and Worship for Guitar	$14.99
00287930	Songs from *A Star Is Born, The Greatest Showman, La La Land,* and More Movie Musicals	$16.99
00702285	Southern Rock Hits	$12.99
00156420	Star Wars Music	$16.99
00121535	30 Easy Celtic Guitar Solos	$16.99
00244654	Top Hits of 2017	$14.99
00283786	Top Hits of 2018	$14.99
00302269	Top Hits of 2019	$14.99
00355779	Top Hits of 2020	$14.99
00374083	Top Hits of 2021	$16.99
00702294	Top Worship Hits	$17.99
00702255	VH1's 100 Greatest Hard Rock Songs	$39.99
00702175	VH1's 100 Greatest Songs of Rock and Roll	$34.99
00702253	Wicked	$12.99

ARTIST COLLECTIONS

00702267	AC/DC for Easy Guitar	$17.99
00156221	Adele – 25	$16.99
00396889	Adele – 30	$19.99
00702040	Best of the Allman Brothers	$16.99
00702865	J.S. Bach for Easy Guitar	$15.99
00702169	Best of The Beach Boys	$16.99
00702292	The Beatles — 1	$22.99
00125796	Best of Chuck Berry	$16.99
00702201	The Essential Black Sabbath	$15.99
00702250	blink-182 — Greatest Hits	$19.99
02501615	Zac Brown Band — The Foundation	$19.99
02501621	Zac Brown Band — You Get What You Give	$16.99
00702043	Best of Johnny Cash	$19.99
00702090	Eric Clapton's Best	$16.99
00702086	Eric Clapton — from the Album Unplugged	$17.99
00702202	The Essential Eric Clapton	$19.99
00702053	Best of Patsy Cline	$17.99
00222697	Very Best of Coldplay – 2nd Edition	$17.99
00702229	The Very Best of Creedence Clearwater Revival	$16.99
00702145	Best of Jim Croce	$16.99
00702278	Crosby, Stills & Nash	$12.99
14042809	Bob Dylan	$15.99
00702276	Fleetwood Mac — Easy Guitar Collection	$17.99
00139462	The Very Best of Grateful Dead	$17.99
00702136	Best of Merle Haggard	$19.99
00702227	Jimi Hendrix — Smash Hits	$19.99
00702288	Best of Hillsong United	$12.99
00702236	Best of Antonio Carlos Jobim	$15.99
00702245	Elton John — Greatest Hits 1970–2002	$19.99
00129855	Jack Johnson	$17.99
00702204	Robert Johnson	$16.99
00702234	Selections from Toby Keith — 35 Biggest Hits	$12.95
00702003	Kiss	$16.99
00702216	Lynyrd Skynyrd	$17.99
00702182	The Essential Bob Marley	$17.99
00146081	Maroon 5	$14.99
00121925	Bruno Mars – Unorthodox Jukebox	$12.99
00702248	Paul McCartney — All the Best	$14.99
00125484	The Best of MercyMe	$12.99
00702209	Steve Miller Band — Young Hearts (Greatest Hits)	$12.95
00124167	Jason Mraz	$15.99
00702096	Best of Nirvana	$17.99
00702211	The Offspring — Greatest Hits	$17.99
00138026	One Direction	$17.99
00702030	Best of Roy Orbison	$17.99
00702144	Best of Ozzy Osbourne	$14.99
00702279	Tom Petty	$17.99
00102911	Pink Floyd	$17.99
00702139	Elvis Country Favorites	$19.99
00702293	The Very Best of Prince	$22.99
00699415	Best of Queen for Guitar	$16.99
00109279	Best of R.E.M.	$14.99
00702208	Red Hot Chili Peppers — Greatest Hits	$19.99
00198960	The Rolling Stones	$17.99
00174793	The Very Best of Santana	$16.99
00702196	Best of Bob Seger	$16.99
00146046	Ed Sheeran	$19.99
00702252	Frank Sinatra — Nothing But the Best	$12.99
00702010	Best of Rod Stewart	$17.99
00702049	Best of George Strait	$17.99
00702259	Taylor Swift for Easy Guitar	$15.99
00359800	Taylor Swift – Easy Guitar Anthology	$24.99
00702260	Taylor Swift — Fearless	$14.99
00139727	Taylor Swift — 1989	$19.99
00115960	Taylor Swift — Red	$16.99
00253667	Taylor Swift — Reputation	$17.99
00702290	Taylor Swift — Speak Now	$16.99
00232849	Chris Tomlin Collection – 2nd Edition	$14.99
00702226	Chris Tomlin — See the Morning	$12.95
00148643	Train	$14.99
00702427	U2 — 18 Singles	$19.99
00702108	Best of Stevie Ray Vaughan	$17.99
00279005	The Who	$14.99
00702123	Best of Hank Williams	$15.99
00194548	Best of John Williams	$14.99
00702228	Neil Young — Greatest Hits	$17.99
00119133	Neil Young — Harvest	$16.99

Prices, contents and availability subject to change without notice.

HAL•LEONARD®

Visit Hal Leonard online at halleonard.com